Notes
From The
Edge
Of The
Narrative
Matrix

For those who look with both eyes.

Contents

Contents

What Is The Narrative Matrix?

In the movie *The Matrix*, humans are imprisoned in a virtual world by a powerful artificial intelligence system in a dystopian future. What they take to be reality is actually a computer program that has been jacked into their brains to keep them in a comatose state. They live their whole lives in that virtual simulation, without any way of knowing that what they appear to be experiencing with their senses is actually made of AI-generated code.

Life in our current society is very much the same. The difference is that instead of AI, it's psychopathic oligarchs who are keeping us asleep in the matrix. And instead of code, it's narrative.

Society is made of narrative like the matrix is made of code. Identity, language, etiquette, social roles, opinions, ideology, religion, ethnicity, philosophy, agendas, rules, laws, money, economics, jobs, hierarchies, politics, government, they're all purely mental constructs which exist nowhere outside of the mental noises in our heads. If I asked you to point to your knee you could do so instantly and wordlessly, but if I asked you to point to the economy, for example, the closest you could come is using a bunch of linguistic symbols to point to a group of concepts. To show me the economy, you'd have to tell me a story.

Anyone who has ever experienced a moment of mental stillness knows that without the chatter, none of those things are part of your actual present experience. There is no identity, language, etiquette, social roles, opinions, ideology, religion, ethnicity, philosophy, agendas, rules, laws, money, economics, jobs, hierarchies, politics or government in your experience without the mental chatter about those things. There's not even a "you" anywhere to be found, because it turns out that that's made of narrative, too.

Without mental narrative, nothing is experienced but sensory impressions appearing to a subject with no clear shape or boundaries. The visual and auditory fields, the sensation of air going in and out of the respiratory system, the feeling of the feet on the ground or the bum in the chair. That's it. That's more or less the totality of life minus narrative.

When you add in the mental chatter, however, none of those things tend to occupy a significant amount of interest or attention. Appearances in the visual and auditory field are suddenly divided up and labeled with language, with attention to them determined by whichever threatens or satisfies the various agendas, fears and desires of the conceptual identity construct known as "you". You can go days, weeks, months or years without really noticing the feeling of your respiratory system or your feet on the ground as your interest and attention gets sucked up into a relationship with society that exists solely as narrative.

"Am I good enough? Am I doing the right thing? Oh man, I hope what I'm trying to do works out. I need to make sure I get all my projects done. If I do that one thing first it might save me some time in the long run. Oh there's Ashley, I hate that bitch. God I'm so fat and ugly. If I can just get the things that I want and accomplish my important goals I'll feel okay. Taxes are due soon. What's on TV? Oh it's that idiot. How the hell did he get elected anyway? Everyone who made that happen is a Nazi. God I can't wait for the weekend. I hope everything goes as planned between now and then."

On and on and on and on. Almost all of our mental energy goes into those mental narratives. They dominate our lives. And, for that reason, people who are able to control those narratives are able to control us.

And they do.

•

Most people try to exert some degree of control over those around them. They try to influence how those in their family, social and employment circles think of them by behaving and speaking in a certain way. Family members will spend their lives telling other family members over and over again that they're not as smart/talented/good as they think they are to keep them from becoming too successful and moving away. Romantic partners will be persuaded that they can never leave because no one else will ever love them. To varying degrees, they manipulate the narratives of individuals.

Then there are the people who've figured out that they can actually take their ability to influence the way people think about themselves and their world and turn it into personal profit. Cult leaders convince followers to turn over their entire lives in service to them. Advertisers convince consumers that they have a problem or deficiency that can only be solved with This Exciting New Product™. Ambitious rat race participants learn how to climb the corporate ladder by winning favor with the right people and inflicting small acts of sabotage against their competing peers. Ambitious journalists learn that they progress much further in their careers by advancing narratives that favor the establishment upon which the plutocrats who own the big media companies have built their kingdoms. They manipulate the narratives of groups.

And then, there are the oligarchs. The master manipulators. These corporate kings of the modern world have learned the secret that every ruler since the dawn of civilization has known: whoever controls the narratives that are believed by a society is the controller of that society. Identity, language, etiquette, social roles, opinions, ideology, religion, ethnicity, philosophy, agendas, rules, laws, money, economics, jobs, hierarchies, politics, government: all mental constructs which only influence society to the extent that they are believed and subscribed to by a significant majority of the collective. If you have influence over the things that people believe about those mental constructs, you have influence over society. You rule it. The oligarchs manipulate the narratives of entire societies.

•

This is why there have been book burnings, heretic burnings, and executions for mocking the emperor throughout history: ideas which differ from the dominant narratives about what power is, how money works, who should be in charge and so on are threatening to a ruler's power in the exact same way that an assassin's dagger is. At any time, in any kingdom, the people could have decided to take the crown off of their king's head and place it upon the head of any common beggar and treat him as the new king. And, in every meaningful way, he would be the new king. The only thing preventing this from happening was dominant narratives subscribed to by the society at the time about Divine Right, fealty, loyalty, noble blood and so on. The only thing keeping the crown on a king's head was narrative.

The exact same thing remains true today; the only thing that has changed is the narratives the public subscribe to. Because of what they are taught in school and what the talking heads on their screens tell them about their nation and their government, most people believe that they live in a relatively free democracy where accountable, temporary power is placed in the hands of a select few based on a voting process informed by the unregulated debate of information and ideas. Completely separate from the government, they believe, is an economy whose behavior is determined by the supply and demand of consumers. In reality, economics, commerce and government are fully controlled by an elite class of plutocrats, who also happen to own the media corporations which broadcast the information about the world onto people's screens.

Control the narratives of economics and commerce, and you control economics and commerce. Control the narratives about politics and government, and you control politics and government. This control is used by the controllers to funnel power to the oligarchs, in this way effectively turning society into one giant energy farm for the elite class.

But it is possible to wake up from that narrative matrix.

•

It isn't easy, and it doesn't happen overnight. It takes work. Inner work. And humility. Nobody likes acknowledging that they've been fooled, and the depth and extent to which we've all been fooled is so deeply pervasive it can be tempting to decide that the work is complete far before one is actually free. Mainstream American liberals think they're clear-eyed because they can see the propaganda strings being pulled by Fox and Donald Trump, and mainstream American conservatives think they're clear-eyed because they can see the propaganda strings being pulled by MSNBC and the Democrats, but the propaganda strings on both trace back to the same puppet master. And seeing that is just the beginning.

But, through sincere, humble research and introspection, it is possible to break free of the matrix and see the full extent to which you and everyone you know has been imprisoned by ideas which have been programmed into social consciousness by the powerful. Not just in our adult lives, but ever since our parents began teaching us how to speak, think and relate to the world.

Not just in the modern world, but as far back as history stretches to when the power-serving belief systems of societal structure and religion were promoted by kings and queens of old. All of society, and all of ourselves, and indeed all of the thoughts in our heads, have been shaped by those in power to their benefit. This is the reality that we were born into, and our entire personality structure has been filtered through and shaped by it.

For this reason, escaping from the power-serving propaganda matrix necessarily means becoming a new creature altogether. The ideas, mental habits and ways of relating to the world which were formed in the matrix are only useful for moving around inside of it. In order to relate to life outside of the power-promulgated narratives which comprise the very fabric of society, you've got to create a whole new operating system for yourself in order to move through life independently of the old programming designed to keep you asleep and controlled.

So it's hard work. You'll make a lot of mistakes along the way, just like an infant slowly learning to walk. But, eventually, you get clear of the programming.

And then you're ready to fight.

•

Because at some point in this process, you necessarily come upon a deep, howling rage within. Rage at the oligarchic manipulators of your species, yes, but also rage against manipulation in all its forms. Rage against everyone who has ever tried to manipulate your narrative, to make you believe things about yourself or make other people believe things about you. Rage against anyone who manipulates anyone else to any extent. When your eyes are clear manipulation stands out like a black fly on a white sheet of paper, and your entire system has nothing to offer it but revulsion and rejection.

So you set to work. You set to work throwing all attempts to manipulate you as far away from yourself as possible, and expunging anyone from your life who refuses to stop trying to control your narrative. Advertising, mass media propaganda, establishment academia, everything gets purged from your life that wants to pull you back into the matrix.

And they will try to pull you back in. Because our narratives are so interwoven and interdependent with everyone else's, and so inseparable from our sense of ourselves, your rejection of the narrative matrix will present as an existential threat to many of your friends and loved ones. You will see many people you used to trust, many of them very close to you, suddenly transform into a bunch of Agent Smiths right in front of your eyes, and they will shame you, guilt you, throw every manipulation tool they have at you to get you to plug the jack back into your brain. But because your eyes are clear, you'll see it all. You won't be fooled.

And then all you'll want is to tear down the matrix from its very foundations and plunge its controllers into irrelevance. You will set to work bringing down the propaganda prison that they have built up around your fellow humans in any way you can, bolt by bolt if you have to, because you know from your own experience that we are all capable of so much more than the puny gear-turning existence they've got everyone churning away at. You will despise the oligarchs for the obscene sacrilege that they have inflicted upon human majesty out of greed and insecurity, and you will make a mortal enemy of the entire machine that they have used to enslave our species.

And, because their entire kingdom is built upon maintaining the illusion of freedom and democracy, all they will have to fight back against you is narrative. They'll try to shame you into silence by calling you a conspiracy theorist, they'll have their media goons and manipulators launch smear campaigns against you, but because your eyes are clear, none of that will work. They've got one weapon, and it doesn't work on you.

And you will set to work waking up humanity from the lie factory, using whatever skills you have, weakening trust in the mass media propaganda machine and opening eyes to new possibilities. And while doing so, you will naturally shine big and bright so the others can find you. And together, we'll not only smash the narratives that imprison us like a human caterpillar swallowing the narrative bullshit and forcing it into the mouth of the next slave, but we'll also create new narratives, better narratives, healthier narratives, for ourselves and for each other, about how the world is and what we want it to be.

Because here's the thing: since it's all narrative, anything is possible. Those who see this have the ability to plunge toward health and human thriving without any regard for the made-up reasons why such a thing is impossible, and plant seeds of light which sprout in unprecedented directions that never could have been predicted by someone plugged into to establishment how-it-is stories. Together, we can determine how society will be. We can re-write the rules. We are re-writing the rules. It's begun already.

Out of the white noise of a failing propaganda machine, a new world is being born, one that respects the autonomy of the individual and their right to self-determination. One that respects our right to collaborate on large scales to create beautiful, healthy, helpful systems without the constant sabotage and disruption of a few power-hungry psychopaths who would rather rule than live. One that respects our right to channel human ingenuity into harmony and human thriving instead of warfare and greed. One that respects our right to take what we need, not just to survive but to thrive, and return it to the earth for renewal. One that respects the sovereign boundaries of not just ourselves and each other, but of the planet spaceship that we live in.

Unjack your cortex fully from the fear-soaked narratives of insanity, and let the true beauty of our real world flood your senses. Let the grief of what we have unknowingly done send you crashing to your knees in sorrow. And when you're ready, stand up. We have much work to do.

Power And Narrative Control

In Tolkien's Middle Earth, the affairs of men are dominated by a cabal of wizards who understand the esoteric art of using language to manipulate reality in a way that advantages powerful rulers —

Oh wait sorry that's regular earth I was thinking of. That's what happens here.

•

Some conspiracy-type people say the world is messed up because we're ruled by illuminati or reptilians, but I'm way more out there than that: I say our entire society is made of imaginary thought stories with little relation to objective reality, and some clever manipulators have figured out how to exploit this.

•

The real underlying currency of our world is not gold, nor bureaucratic fiat, nor even military might. The real underlying currency of our world is narrative, and the ability to control it. Everything always comes down to this one real currency. If you look at what all these think tanks, NGOs, media outlets and grant making networks that billionaires pour their money into actually do, it ultimately boils down to controlling the dominant stories that people tell about what's going on in their world.

•

Real change won't come until people rise up. People won't rise up as long as they're successfully propagandized. People will remain successfully propagandized until they evolve minds which can't be manipulated. Our world will change when our relationship with narrative changes.

•

Most of humanity's problems boil down to an unhealthy relationship with narrative. Individually our suffering ensues from believed mental narratives about self, other and world, and collectively our destructive behaviors are driven by the propaganda narratives of the powerful.

Most people's lives are dominated by mental story, so whoever can control those stories controls the people. The good news is that all we need to do to reclaim our world from the controllers is to reclaim our stories. The barrier between us and freedom is as thin as a fairy tale.

•

The world is messed up because powerful people think in terms of narrative control, and ordinary people don't. Change that and you change the world.

•

The three most overlooked and under-appreciated aspects of the human condition are (1) consciousness itself, (2) the way compulsive thought patterns shape our experience and our lives, and (3) the effects of mass media propaganda. In that order.

•

The primary reason people are so vulnerable to propaganda is that hardly anyone clearly sees just how much human consciousness is dominated by mental narrative. There's a night and day difference between reality and the stories minds tell about reality. Manipulators exploit this.

Most people assume that the mental stories in their heads are an accurate reflection of what's happening outside their skull, and that simply isn't the case. Manipulators know they can just feed people stories—narratives—about what's happening and they'll accept those narratives as reality.

Manipulators know they can trade a bunch of convincing words in exchange for all sorts of real valuables: money, sex, deals, loyalty, votes, political power. Humanity's deluded relationship with narrative means you can get real, concrete treasures in exchange for pure illusion.

Most of the things which consume your attention are pure narrative constructs: religion, philosophy, culture, politics, the economy, even what you take to be your very self. But few ever take the time to sift these narratives apart from reality, so we're hackable by manipulators.

The difference between what's happening and what the babbling mind says is happening could not possibly be more different. Until our species evolves a new relationship with mental narrative which allows a real relationship with the real world, we'll keep moving toward extinction.

•

For as long as there has been language and power there have been narratives circulating to advantage the powerful. Much of our so-called "culture" is just ancient power-serving proto-propaganda deliberately interwoven into our ancestors' worldviews.

•

If people truly understood the extent to which mental narrative dominates their experience of life, propaganda, advertising and all other forms of psychological manipulation would be regarded by our society similarly to physical assault or property theft.

•

Propaganda is the root of all our problems; people consent to inequality and injustice because they're manipulated into doing so. And propaganda is only effective because we've got an idiotic societal taboo against acknowledging that we can be fooled. That our minds are hackable.

Manipulation only works when you don't know it's happening. Those who think they're too clever to be manipulated (which would be the majority of people) are the most vulnerable to manipulation. If we just made manipulation more shameful than being manipulated, this could change.

You cannot form an accurate worldview without accounting for the fact that powerful people have invested a great deal in manipulating that worldview, and that to some extent they have probably succeeded. Because being manipulated is considered shameful, most don't look at this.

I have been manipulated and fooled. So have you. It happens to all of us. There's no shame in it. The shame belongs solely to those doing the manipulating and deceiving. Fraud is a crime for a reason, and the one they charge for that crime is not the victim, it's the perpetrator.

Conmen will always try to convince you that it's your fault you were conned. If they can do that, they get away with the con. This is true of all manipulators, and it's why you should never blame the gullible. Being gullible isn't a crime, being a conman is.

•

Nobody who is being successfully manipulated is free, and our world is dominated by mass-scale manipulation. It doesn't matter how many "rights" you have on paper, if you've been manipulated into supporting or consenting to the agendas of power you might as well be in a cage.

As long as the powerful are propagandizing the people, the people aren't truly operating with free will. Anyone who's escaped a relationship with a manipulative abuser understands that you're not really operating with much free agency while you're being psychologically dominated.

•

Manipulation is a necessary component in long-term abusive relationships, because people don't tend to stay in abusive situations unless they're manipulated into it. This is true whether you're talking about significant others or globe-spanning power structures.

•

People have been manipulating each other since the invention of language and manipulating each other at mass scale since the invention of government. All that's changed is the mass scale has gotten much larger and the manipulation much more sophisticated.

•

The world would be so much better if everyone just watched people's actions and ignored their stories about their actions. It would radically change politics, it would prevent abusive relationships, it would stifle manipulators, and it would transform human civilization.

•

If you ever feel unimportant, remember that rich and powerful people are constantly pouring effort and wealth into trying to manipulate the thoughts in your head.

•

Hi I'm Sleazy McPundit with WMD News. To explain why more internet censorship is needed to fight disinformation, here's a panel of millionaires who are paid to lie to you.

•

The mainstream worldview isn't mainstream because it is more fact-based, logical, or makes better arguments than other potential worldviews, it's mainstream because vast fortunes are poured into keeping it mainstream.

•

Mainstream news is just advertising. You watch advertisements for maintaining the plutocratic status quo, then you watch advertisements between those advertisements for useless crap to make plutocrats even richer. It's all just different layers of marketing. When I was getting my journalism degree they used to talk about journos selling their souls and going into marketing, going into PR. It's like, bitch, you're already doing that.

•

Without extensive marketing it would never occur to you that Mountain Dew is something you should put inside your body or that endless war is something you should accept as normal.

•

War is the worst thing in the world. By far. If the rank-and-file public could see past the veil of propaganda and distortion and objectively see war for the horrific thing that it is, ending it would immediately become everyone's foremost priority. Hence all the war propaganda.

•

It's such a trip how opposition to mass-scale murder and oppression is the single most self-evidently correct position anyone could possibly take, yet so few take that position in a clear and unequivocal way. The reason is of course generations of propaganda brainwashing.

Nobody comes out of the womb demanding to go to war. Left unmolested it would never occur to a normal human brain that strangers on the other side of the planet need to have explosives dropped on them by overpriced aircraft. The problem isn't people democratically voting for warmongers and consenting to military mass murder of their own free will, the problem is propaganda.

•

People only ever think you're wrong to reject mainstream politics and media because they have no idea how fucked things really are.

•

It only takes a rudimentary understanding of human psychology to manipulate someone. Edward Bernays was recruited by the US government to study the science of modern propaganda in 1917. This science has been in research and development for over a century. Don't underestimate its power.

•

Propaganda is so advanced that rank-and-file members of the public will openly cheerlead their government's imprisonment of Assange so that their government can continue to lie to them.

•

The dawn of political insight is when you realize propaganda isn't just something that is done by other countries and other political parties.

•

To be a real journalist you must ask inconvenient questions, shine light in inconvenient directions, refuse to parrot establishment narratives, and be indifferent to the approval of the powerful.

To be a rich and famous journalist, you must do the exact opposite of these things.

•

Step 1: Be the billionaire class.

Step 2: Buy up all news media.

Step 3: Structure outlets to elevate voices who defend the status quo.

Step 4: Smear non-plutocratic media who don't protect the status quo as crazy conspiracy theorists and Russian propaganda.

Step 5: Dominate the narrative about what's going on in the world.

•

"Those Chinese sure have an evil oppressive government," said the guy whose government robs its citizens to violently destroy disobedient nations around the world, made possible by a one-party political system and the most sophisticated propaganda engine ever made.

•

The most influential news outlets in the western world uncritically parrot whatever they're told to say by the most powerful and depraved intelligence agencies on the planet, then tell you that Russia and China are bad because they have state media.

•

The difference between state media and western media is that in state media the government controls what information the public is given about what's going on in the world in order to prevent political dissent, whereas in western media this is instead done by billionaires.

•

There are exactly zero babies in the mainstream media bathwater. It's a propaganda network which manufactures consent for mass murder, oppression and exploitation, and it deserves nothing other than total obliteration. Toss it all out.

•

Reading The New York Times to learn about what's happening in the world is like reading Calvin and Hobbes to learn about tigers.

•

Whenever anyone annoys dominant power structures, the political/media class instantly becomes very interested in informing us how horrible that person is. You see this with anti-establishment candidates, you see it with anti-empire national leaders, you see it with whistleblowers, and you see it with leak publishers.

•

Russian, adjective

Meaning: Accurate, in accordance with known facts about reality.

E.g. "Saying the US armed terrorists in Syria is a Russian talking point."

"There's Russian online chatter saying the Democratic primary is rigged."

"WikiLeaks is a Russian asset."

Synonyms: true, factual, correct

•

Robert A. Heinlein said "Man is not a rational animal; he is a rationalizing animal." We act based on untold millennia of conditioning, then tell stories about why that action makes sense. This is as true of empires as it is of individuals. Mainstream narratives are rationalizations.

Imperialist elites are ultimately no more clued-in on why they do what they do than anyone else. They're acting out the same evolutionary, cultural and personal conditioning as the rest of us—essentially just the seeking of security and control—and then telling fancy stories.

It could have just as easily gone any other direction. If things had been a bit different and Mexico had wound up being the unipolar hegemon and Saudi Arabia had refused to comply with its interests, all our plutocratic media would be calling for sanctions and explaining to us in Spanish why the House of Saud must go. If the interests of power were served by everyone wearing tinfoil on their heads, the oligarchic media would spend all their time explaining why that's necessary and everyone should do it. The rationalizations come after the primitive impulses to act.

•

"Man is not a rational animal; he is a rationalizing animal" is also apparent in the effects of mass media psyops; people think they hate an empire-targeted nation/person because of reasons X, Y and Z, but really it's because the empire targeted them, and then propagandists rationalized it.

If people were really honest with themselves, they'd say "You know I think I hate that Official Bad Guy of the Day because of reasons X, Y and Z, but maybe it's actually because he began inconveniencing the empire, and for that reason the media started telling me to hate him?" But generally they don't, because it's uncomfortable admitting to yourself that you have not been thinking rationally; that you have actually been rationalizing the entirely irrational behavior of a depraved empire without realizing it, just because some pundits told you to.

•

There are two kinds of journalists: those who present themselves as unbiased reporters of objective factual reality, and those who are honest.

•

It's weird how many analysts in both alternative and mainstream media get by on using esoteric buzzwords, obscure references and complex concepts in order to sound intelligent. If only a few people can understand you that doesn't make you smart, it makes you bad at your job.

•

Many believe that the mass media just tell whole-cloth, outright lies all the time, but that's not usually how it works. What they do is selectively omit inconvenient facts, disproportionately amplify convenient facts, and uncritically report on dubious government assertions. Basically they only tell the truth when it's convenient for them, and when it's inconvenient they are silent. Only telling the truth when it's convenient for you is effectively the same as lying all the time, but you can get away with it a lot easier.

●

Mainstream media outlets which publish anonymous intelligence claims with no proof are just publishing CIA press releases disguised as news.

●

The fact that mainstream news outlets consistently refuse to account for something as basic and indisputable as intelligence agencies being known liars should by itself fully discredit the entire institution of mass news reporting.

●

Really it's not that there are a bunch of mainstream news reporters who are knowingly and deliberately deceiving you. It's that in order to become a mainstream news reporter, you need to plug your whole mind into an entire power-serving worldview that is not remotely based in truth.

●

As long as dissent is relegated to the fringes, there is no actual free speech. Saying you have free speech because you're allowed to make blogs or Youtube videos is like saying you have free speech because you can dig a hole in the ground and say whatever you want into it.

We have a media system which creates an inverse correlation between one's access to influential platforms and how dissident their speech is. Allowing people free speech which has zero meaningful impact is not allowing free speech at all.

●

Part of the problem is that the most influential voices are people for whom the status quo has worked out well. Celebrities. Politicians. Pundits. Plutocrats. If you look at them, you'd think everything is basically fine. Meanwhile those who've been crushed by existing systems are voiceless, which creates the illusion that those systems work.

●

The official function of outlets like Voice of America and Radio Free Asia is to administer US propaganda. Their unofficial function is to promote the idea that they are the only outlets which administer US propaganda.

●

Those who say Russia can influence an election with a few tweets and Facebook memes are implicitly admitting that the media-owning plutocratic class necessarily has many orders of magnitude more control over their political system.

●

If you find yourself thinking more thoughts about China's authoritarian government than about the abusive authoritarian governments of US allies like Saudi Arabia, Israel, Turkey, Egypt, the Philippines etc, it's because you've been propagandized to align you with US interests.

•

It's not the most famous mainstream media lies that do the most damage. It's the little ones they tell many time every day via spin, omission, half-truth and distortion which cause everyone to accept the idea that this bat shit crazy status quo is normal and inescapable.

•

Mainstream media reporters have a much higher body count than all serial killers and terrorist organizations combined. They do not deserve respect, and their institutions should not exist.

•

A problem whose solution entails the deployment of US troops, bombs or weapons is almost certainly a made-up problem.

•

Think tanks are institutions which pay academics to think up reasons why it would be smart and good to do something evil and stupid, then insert those reasons into key points of influence. Mainstream media cites them as authorities on foreign policy because mainstream media is propaganda.

"Think tank" is a great and accurate label. Not because a great deal of thought happens in them, but because they're dedicated to controlling what people think, and because they are artificial enclosures made for slimy creatures.

•

Never use the word "whore" to refer to a sex worker; they earn an honest and respectable living and they shouldn't be demeaned for it. That word should only ever be used for members of the political/media class.

•

Hollywood is the single most heartless, artless, unfeeling cesspool of sociopathy on planet earth, and humanity would greatly benefit from ceasing to get its culture from there.

•

A propaganda machine that can make people worry about foreign governments while their own government is destroying lives in their own country and all over the world is a propaganda machine that can make people believe anything.

•

If online censorship keeps tightening, the internet will cease to be an information-democratizing tool of the people to any extent at all and will instead just enable ruling power structures to administer propaganda much more quickly and efficiently than they could previously.

•

A news outlet which does not constantly inform its audience of all their government's misdeeds around the world is not a news outlet.

•

The mass media don't use the word "moderate" accurately, whether they're talking about moderate rebels in Syria or moderates who stand between two warmongering oligarchic parties. This is because the mass media are there to promote an empire whose ideology is violent extremism.

•

Governments make evidence-free claims which the mass media report uncritically, with ordinary citizens expected to either prove them wrong or shut up and believe. The burden of proof is fallaciously placed on members of the public and tiny indie media outlets with no resources to disprove the claims, instead of on massive news media outlets with abundant wealth and resources. It should be the exact opposite: with unproven government claims ignored until hard proof is provided, and with mass media reporters doing their goddamn jobs.

•

Truth is the first casualty in war. This adage is especially true of cold war, where the absence of hot firepower makes an emphasis on mass-scale psychological operations necessary.

•

So many problems would disappear if news outlets would just stick to reporting known, verified information instead of unproven government claims, dumbass Russia conspiracy theories, and opinions by pundits who support imperialism and oligarchy.

It would fix most of what's wrong if our institutions just did what they claim they do. If the media actually told people the truth about what's happening and votes actually enacted the will of the electorate, you'd have an educated populace shaping their world based on truth.

The problem is not the official system, the problem is that the official system is a lie. A lie used to propagandize and deceive the public into thinking they're not being fucked over by unelected oligarchs and opaque government agencies bent on world conquest.

•

If you were sent to a foreign civilization to report on what they do, you would slowly start absorbing their language, culture and customs, and gradually their strange ways would become the norm for you. Anyway, that's what goes wrong with journalists who report on politicians.

•

The plutocrat-owned western political/media class has built up a collective doctrine that you cannot simply end overseas wars and bring the troops home, and that anyone who says you can is a lunatic. That's all it is though: fact-free religious doctrine, espoused on blind faith.

When it comes to large-scale governing and international matters, the mainstream perspective is only mainstream because extremely wealthy people poured vast fortunes into making it mainstream. There's no collective wisdom or truth in it, it's just what power wants us to believe about what's going on.

•

It's such a delicate balancing act that US news media walk each day, having to tell people that mass murder is perfectly fine over and over and over again and then pretending to give a shit when mass shootings happen.

•

Mainstream media opinion segments are toxic and shouldn't exist. Not because expression of opinion is wrong but because they only ever platform (at most) two mainstream ideological positions arguing over the specifics of how, not if, the agendas of oligarchs and government agencies should be advanced.

Mass media "news" segments tell you what to think. Mass media "opinion" segments tell you how to think. It's a complete training program.

Mass media "news" parrots government lies about what's happening in the world and only gives you information which benefits establishment power structures, then mass media "opinion" segments train you on how to incorporate that extremely distorted information into your ideological belief system.

•

Those who advance war propaganda are participating in that war just as much as the people who actually go and fight in it. They're just playing a much safer and more cowardly role.

The deployment of a bomb or missile doesn't begin when a pilot pushes a button, it begins when propaganda narratives used to promote those operations start circulating in public attention. If you help circulate war propaganda, you're as complicit as the one who pushes the button.

Capitalism Is Killing Us

Q: What is capitalism?

A: Capitalism is a wonderful political/economic system which has given us powerful technology, a wide assortment of breakfast cereals, and near term human extinction.

•

Capitalism is literally a game. It's based on completely made-up rules with a completely made-up points system just like any other game. The only difference between this game and the others is this one gets taken so seriously that losing can kill you in real life.

•

Ecocide will be a problem as long as ecocide remains profitable. War will be a problem as long as war remains profitable. Politicians will cater to profit-seeking sociopaths as long as profit determines what drives human behavior.

•

All the most profitable activities involve inflicting trauma of some sort. War, monopolism, usury, strip mining, fossil fuels, factory farming, ads convincing us we're deficient, etc. We'll traumatize our planet bare if human behavior remains driven by profit and competition.

Nothing but a complete global truce on this front will suffice. Nations become extremely powerful by excelling at profit and subsuming anyone who doesn't, to the point where even nations which don't worship profit are forced to pursue it out of self-defense.

What we need now is to slow down, turn around, and begin collaborating with each other and our ecosystem. But pursuit of profit is inherently opposed to this. We're crushing our ecosystem and each other in a mad rat race toward extinction. We must turn and go the opposite way.

•

Any system which allows people with wealth/power to have more influence over news media, ideas and information than ordinary people will always necessarily lead to authoritarianism. If you want actual equality and freedom, you need to pry narrative control from the hands of the wealthy and powerful and make it fully democratized.

•

Saying "It's not capitalism that's the problem, it's corporatism!" is the same as saying "It's not smoking that's my problem, it's the emphysema!"

•

Capitalism will always necessarily lead to authoritarianism, because cutthroat dominators will always be the ones to rise to the top of any capitalist system.

There's this notion that those who rise to the top of capitalism are not only as good as normal people, but actually better. And of course the exact opposite is true: those who rise to the top of capitalist systems are those who are sociopathic enough to do anything to get ahead.

Billionaires are not good stewards of society. They are not kind. They are not wise. They aren't even really smart. They just figured out how to diddle narratives and numbers in a way that funnels them money and power. They are empty parasitic middle-men, and they are conmen.

•

Money is power. Power is relative. Sociopaths seek money to obtain wealth/power and are incentivized to bring down the relative wealth/power of everyone else. This is why the saying "a rising tide lifts all boats" doesn't work in real life; someone's drilling holes in all the other boats.

This is why you see political pushes toward economic justice aggressively thwarted in the most powerful government on earth. The people on top are using their wealth as political influence to keep everyone else down, because money is power and power is relative. If everyone is king then no one is king.

In a system of capitalism/competition, sociopaths always win, since they're the ones who are willing to do anything to get ahead. Once they're ahead they're motivated to keep everyone else down. The narrative that competition and the rat race uplifts everyone is necessarily false, because the rats who climb to the top of the rope have every incentive to cut it behind them. Everything they value is offered as an incentive to keep everyone else from succeeding.

Capitalists argue the real problem is too much government, which plutocrats can manipulate to gain more power. But even if we eliminated government altogether and went full ancap, wealth would still give you a huge power edge and power would still be relative, maintaining this same dynamic. A very wealthy person will necessarily have more power than someone with very little wealth, regardless of how much government you have.

It's impossible to design a system where one can obtain way more wealth than anyone else and not be incentivized to, and capable of, sabotaging everyone behind them to expand their own relative power. Some sort of collaborative model is the only way our species survives.

•

Capitalism will let you starve to death while sitting meters away from food.

•

We are bulldozing a paradise while praying we go to Heaven when we die. We are killing off giant-brained leviathans in our own oceans whose mental lives we know little about while searching the stars for intelligent life. We are burning our home in our search for a sense of home.

•

Our species is never going to compete its way out of the existential threats it competed its way into. We will move out of the capitalist model of competition and into a collaborative relationship with each other and with our ecosystem, or we will go extinct. It is that simple.

•

How to solve the climate crisis:

– End the economic system which requires infinite growth on a finite planet.

– Let people get more relaxed and less busy.

– End corporate influence in politics.

– End militarism.

– End patents.

– Kill the capitalist propaganda engine known as the mainstream media.

•

Removing profit-seeking as a driving force of human behavior would end the artificial creation of demand for planet-destroying bullshit that people don't need, and open up the possibility of planet-healing action that capitalism does not and cannot value.

•

Those who talk about how much capitalism has done for the world while ignoring the fact that it's killing the ecosystem are like proponents of a miraculous new cancer treatment which shrinks tumors like nothing else and its only side effect is that it kills the patient.

•

The ecosystem is dying because it is vastly more profitable to destroy the ecosystem than to preserve it. Capitalism offers no solutions for this, only exacerbation. We're not going to consume our way out of this. That's why hardcore capitalists just pretend it's not happening.

⁕

The single worst polluter in the world? The US war machine. People calling for climate action without calling to defund the Pentagon do not actually care about climate action.

⁕

Environmentalism which adamantly ignores the need for a complete overhaul of the economic system which created this mess is just feel-good PR for capitalism.

⁕

Trying to solve the climate crisis with plutocrat-driven tech consumption is like trying to put out a house fire with a flamethrower.

⁕

A species that is hurtling toward extinction has no business promoting slow incremental change.

If your ideology requires slow incremental change, it's not an ideology. It's a pastime while waiting for armageddon.

⁕

That the wealthy exploit the working class is an outrage. That they continually restructure all of society around that exploitation is a crime.

•

If an individual has been caught using a weapon to harm members of society, then society is justified in forcibly disarming that individual in self-defense. This is true whether the individual's weapon is a knife, a gun, or billions of dollars.

•

Billionaires are just thieves who commit state-authorized thievery.

•

Not every predator is a billionaire, but every billionaire is a predator.

•

Steal from the wealthy and give a bit to your friend and they'll call you a thief. Steal from the working class and give a bit to agendas you approve of and they'll call you a philanthropist.

•

How to be a billionaire philanthropist:

1. Steal all the money from everyone else.

2. Share a tiny amount of it, if and when it makes you feel good about yourself.

3. Receive massive worldwide accolades for your generosity and have many large buildings named after you.

•

Wealth is just the dumb luck of finding yourself on the receiving point of inheritance, privilege, and a system set up to reward manipulative middle men instead of laborers, all of which have their roots in some point in history where some asshole stole some land from the people who lived there before him.

•

Back when the wealthy had less wealth and ordinary citizens could support a family on a single income, the rich had a concept called "noblesse oblige" meaning their status came with obligations to society. Now the wealth gap is much greater, and the rich feel no obligation to anyone.

•

The capitalism cultist's solution to caring for developmentally disabled children is that their families care for them at home for their entire lives. Society gets those families' labor, for free.

Free stuff! Sweet, huh? But the problem with capitalism is that eventually you run out of other people's free labor.

•

Arguably the only people who actually truly understand the highly unscientific and completely made-up field of economics are those who manipulate the economy for their own benefit. And they only understand it because they're the ones authoring its self-fulfilling prophecies.

•

Anyone who claims the left is starting a "class war" is claiming that the billionaire class has not already been waging war on normal people on a multitude of fronts for many years. They're saying that the exploitation, oppression, manipulation, corruption and poverty is all in your imagination.

•

Whenever there's an economic downturn I always get my hopes up that maybe this is the one where people go "Hey wait a minute, this whole 'economy' thing is made up! We can just make up something different instead!"

•

Believing people can learn to self-govern in healthy collaboration with each other and with their ecosystem is infinitely more sane and rational than believing the world's problems will be solved by greedy tech oligarchs.

•

"The poor should just work harder to become self-sufficient like me," said the man whose entire way of life is built on foreign slave labor.

•

You don't need any talent or skills to obtain extreme wealth, just find a way to insert yourself as an unnecessary middleman between consumers and talented/skillful people and then siphon off most of the profits.

•

Me, a naive idiot: The world can be saved by a mass-scale shift in human consciousness into a healthy relationship with mental narrative.

Smart, realistic person: No that's stupid and impractical. The world will be saved by monopolistic profit-chasing tech oligarchs.

•

Capitalism will keep getting more and more unjust and exploitative until people force its end. You can try making it about elite globalist conspiracies and corrupt governments all you want, but ultimately it's really just capitalism following its natural and inevitable course.

This is why I often avoid making our world's problems about specific individuals; our world's problems are not about specific individuals. You could get rid of all the individuals currently screwing us and if you kept the same systems they'd be replaced almost instantly.

People whose ideology prohibits them from admitting capitalism is responsible for humanity's existential crises need to make up other reasons for those crises — It's the globalists. It's the Jews. It's corrupt politicians. No, it's just capitalism doing what capitalism has to do. There are no specific groups or individuals you could eliminate from the equation to make capitalism move in a healthy way. As long as depravity is profitable and human behavior is driven by profit, humanity will always necessarily follow a depraved trajectory.

This doesn't mean criticisms of individuals are invalid, they're just not striking the root. Get rid of all the elites poisoning the world today and if you leave the same systems in place we'll find ourselves getting screwed by the Whateverski family and some guy named O'Donnell.

So many of the popular theories in today's conspiracy circles ultimately boil down to "Oh no, the elites are ruining the capitalism!"

No they're not. They are perfectly embodying it.

•

The focus shouldn't just be on bad things done by individual plutocrats – Gates did X, Bezos did Y, etc. The primary focus should be on how we shouldn't have a system which allows *any* individual to have that much power over our world. No individual should have that much power to do that much harm.

•

You couldn't create a more perfect profit-generating scheme than war. Entire civilizations can be streamlined into the task of cranking out top-of-the-line, name-brand killing machines at the drop of a false flag.

•

If you want more of something, apply capitalism; if you want less of something, apply socialism. Capitalism is great for making a ton of stuff, but for making less stuff it's shit, whether that be making less illness, less pollution, less ecocide, less war, fewer prisoners, etc. Right now we live in a world that needs a great reduction of a great many things, and there's just no way to get there as long as human behavior is driven by profit.

This is obviously true of things like healthcare, where actually eliminating illness kills demand. But it's also true of even things like charity programs, where if you fix the problem people are throwing money at then a lot of professionals lose their income sources. You've got to incentivize people to disappear the problems, but capitalism doesn't have an effective way of disappearing things. It necessarily incentivizes people to perpetuate them.

This is just common sense business practice that anyone who's ever run a business should understand. If you make products, your goal is to create and sell as many products as possible. If you sell services, your goal is to create as many clients as possible. So if your business is war machinery, you will necessarily be incentivized to lobby for as many wars as possible. If your business is medicine, you will be incentivized to keep as many sick people around as possible. As long as we're motivated by profit, such things persist.

Trying to consume our way out of our current predicament is like trying to eat your way into weight loss.

•

Since the dawn of history the true purpose of religion has been to shape societies, dominate civilizations and build entire empires, whether that religion is called "Christianity", "Islam", or "economics".

•

Rags-to-riches stories of people clawing their way to the top from nothing are just the modern day equivalent of fairy tales about peasants discovering they're actually royalty: wildly improbable fantasies to let the commoners imagine the system could one day work for them, too.

●

You can have anxiety without being poor but you can't be poor without anxiety. If you want to solve the mental health crisis, start by making sure people have enough money to function.

●

Mainstream feminism neglects the injustices of motherhood to a truly embarrassing extent. It's become a movement to ensure that women have as much of a right as men to facilitate all the sickest aspects of patriarchy, while mothers everywhere are constantly forced to choose between economic hardship and staying with awful partners as they're smashed with medieval judgmental attitudes about their parenting decisions.

●

Space colonization will never happen and can never happen. People mistakenly believe it's possible for the same reason we're killing our environment: we egotistically imagine that we are separable from the ecosystemic context in which we evolved.

People who think humans can live separately from earth's ecosystem simply haven't looked closely enough at what precisely a human is and what an illusion our separateness is. We'll never attain time travel and we'll never colonize space. They are goals with illusory premises.

The closest we've ever come to space colonization is glorified scuba expeditions, where supplies are brought in from our native environment. And this is as close as we'll get (with perhaps some relative advancement), because the human organism will never be a separate entity. The closest we'll ever come is extending our ecosystem a bit beyond its natural boundaries by carrying finite parts of it out with us.

Space colonization isn't impossible due to some limitation on the potential of technological innovation, but because of a fundamental misunderstanding of what the human organism is and its relationship to its ecosystem. People believe space colonization is possible because they believe, erroneously, that we're separate from earth in some way.

We're not separate from the planet, and we never will be. We're connected to our ecosystems in innumerable highly complex ways. You have an entire ecosystem in your guts with its own relationship with the outer ecosystem, to name one of many possible examples.

Believing you can use technology to extract a human organism and send it to a separate space colony with its own artificial ecosystem is like believing you can extract a ripple from the pond in which it's appearing, or believing technology will someday enable your shadow to run around separately from your body. We are just not nearly as separate and separable as conventional minds imagine.

The unspoken assumption behind the infinite growth required by capitalism is that we can expand into space and explore the stars, and we just can't. That's a delusion arising from a fundamental misperception of what a human organism is. We're destroying our home like idiots while looking to space for salvation, and we simply will never live there.

We're just going to have to learn to live here.

•

The main thing billionaires get out of having a space program is a narrative management op which helps market their insane economic doctrine of infinite growth on a finite planet; it doesn't matter what the billionaire class does to our home because we can all just move to space. They have to know on some level that their stated goals for space won't actually happen before their economic doctrine turns our planet into toxic landfill, but they need to spin the idea of space colonization or we'd stop their rapacious expansionism.

•

The ego says "You can't dispense with me; I am you, I am your true nature, without me you will fail."

Capitalism says "You can't dispense with me; I am you, I am your true nature, without me you will fail."

Both are liars.

Both are impostors.

Both are sickness posing as health.

The Empire

I'll never get used to the fact that I focus my attention on the most powerful and deadly government on the face of the earth, and people are so propagandized that they see this as a strange and suspicious thing to do.

Opposing the most destructive behaviors of the most powerful government on earth should not be an unusual and controversial position.

•

I don't criticize governments outside the US-centralized empire for the same reason the world's fattest man doesn't go around telling other people to lose weight. If you're part of a globe-spanning power alliance that is far worse than anyone else, it's gross to point fingers.

•

In old-style British imperialism, they'd invade your country and replace your flag with theirs. In new-style US imperialism, your country keeps its flag, and the takeover can happen so slyly that the nation's citizens sometimes don't even know it's occurred. It's much more efficient.

•

All empires throughout history have had some kind of positive narrative about why it's right that they should be conquering and dominating the world. The US-centralized empire with its bogus "freedom and democracy" schtick is no different.

•

International alliances are often thought of as matters of secondary importance, as just something governments do when possible to make themselves a bit safer, wealthier, etc. Actually, uniting nations into one power structure is the goal, and it's what alliances are really for.

•

On the right they often refer to deaths under 20th century communist governments. On the left they talk a lot about Nazi Germany. What doesn't get nearly enough attention is how the tyrannical force that's doing the killing and oppressing right now is the US-centralized empire.

The killers who are racking up the major body count right now are not the communists, nor the Nazis, nor the Muslims, nor the Russians or the Chinese, but the so-called moderate centrists of the so-called liberal world order that is led by the United States. What our insane society calls "centrists" are actually violent, tyrannical extremists.

Our society fixates on Nazi Germany with such masturbatory fascination because it allows us to pretend that horrific mass-scale evil is just something that was inflicted in the past, by someone else, in another part of the world, and not right here and now by our own government.

•

Kill millions in concentration camps and they'll call you a monster. Kill millions with bombs and they'll call you a moderate.

•

I talk about how outrageous war is a lot because we should all be talking about how outrageous war is all the time. War is the most insane thing people do and the fact that it's actively pursued by the powerful should enrage everyone. Don't ever let them desensitize you to this.

If someone flips out and shoots a bunch of people it's in headlines for days, but if powerful individuals calmly orchestrate the slaughter of many times more people overseas it barely makes the news. This isn't sane or normal, and it's so vital that we remain aware of that.

It's so important not to let them rob you of your humanity by convincing you to ignore imperialist warmongering. Don't let them put cataracts over your eyes and calluses on your heart like that. Mass military violence is a horror that should send shockwaves through your core.

•

In a remotely sane world, war would be the last thing anyone ever wants and would be turned to only as a very last resort. In a world that's dominated by an empire which seeks total planetary control, wars are planned as an ends in themselves and excuses are invented to get into them.

•

The US empire, like any other predator, prioritizes maximum reward for minimum expenditure of energy. It targets small, weak nations with lots of resources to control, ensuring maximum geostrategic control for minimum effort. The ultimate goal, though, is total planetary rule.

•

The US empire is the creepiest thing in the world. It's this smiley faced serial killer monologuing about freedom and democracy and churning out movies about how fun and happy it is while butchering human beings all around the world. The more you think about it the creepier it gets.

•

The impulse to control things is why egos exist. The impulse to control things is also why empires exist.

•

US political leaders are so revered by the media and so normalized on our screens that it's easy to forget how many children they've murdered.

•

My special hatred for US imperialism really got going when I escaped from an abusive relationship which operated in very much the same way: creating the nice-guy illusion of freedom and equality while covertly using manipulation to exploit, oppress, and choke the life out of me.

A dumb abuser dominates like a standard tyrannical dictatorship. A smart abuser dominates like the US empire: using manipulation to make it look fair, like the victim chose it for themselves, while crushing and carving pieces off of them to shape things to the abuser's will.

•

Americans: healthcare please

US government: Sorry did you say more war ships in the South China Sea?

Americans: no, healthcare

US government: Alright, you drive a hard bargain. Here are more war ships in the South China Sea.

•

The US doesn't deprive its people of basic social programs because all its money goes into the war machine, it deprives them because if Americans stopped being so poor, stressed and busy it would become much harder to manufacture their consent for the actions of that war machine.

An entire globe-spanning empire is built on a closed set of eyelids. It depends on the American people not waking up to what's going on in their government, and the imperialists have every incentive in the world to prevent that from happening. US imperialism and economic injustice are linked directly, not indirectly.

•

Many on the left care about domestic policy a lot more than they care about foreign policy. Meanwhile, foreign policy is the foremost priority of the establishment they're trying to take down. This arrangement works out very nicely for the powerful.

•

Saying a US politician is bad on foreign policy but good on domestic policy is a bit like saying "Yeah my boyfriend murders hitchhikers, but he cooks."

•

"Peace through strength" just means "We'll take money away from the poor and the needy and use it to beef up our already bloated military so we can bully the world into obedience." That's not peace, that's tyranny.

•

War is mass murder. Speaking out against it is more important than people's emotional comfort. It's worth disrupting family dinners over. It's worth jeopardizing friendships over. History won't look kindly on those who chose silent complicity over anti-imperialism.

•

"That dictator kills his own people!" said the empire that constantly kills its own people.

•

The US outsources all its ugliest aspects so that American voters don't have to look at them. It outsources its torture. It outsources its slavery. It outsources its wars. It outsources the holding cells for its political prisoners.

•

Here's a crazy thought: if "the troops" are constantly feeling the need to commit suicide after doing what they've been ordered to do while deployed, maybe what they're doing over there isn't so great and noble after all.

•

No US soldier has died for any reason that could be described as heroic, or even justifiable, for generations. We simply do not have a world order where such a thing happens anymore. They only ever die defending the interests of corporations and depraved government agencies.

•

Schrodinger's superpower: America is simultaneously (A) an unstoppable military and economic force that ought to be in charge of the entire world, and (B) the poor widdle victim of some big, mean bully on the other side of the planet.

•

Imagine living in Nazi Germany and tut-tutting about Jim Crow laws in the American south while ignoring the horrific abuses of your own country. That's what it's like when people who live in the US-centralized empire focus on the alleged misdeeds of non-aligned nations.

•

Mentally mute the narrative soundtrack about things changing drastically between US presidents, and what you see is a government continuing along pretty much the exact same trajectory with only cosmetic changes between administrations. World minus narrative is night-and-day different from world plus narrative.

•

Wars aren't good vs evil; usually they're geostrategic agenda vs geostrategic agenda. But Hollywood always portrays war as good vs evil, which is why empire apologists always bleat "You're saying Dictator X is a Good Guy!" whenever you oppose interventionism in X targeted nation.

Without that conditioning by professional storytellers, it would never occur to us to try and find the "good guys" in the chaos of a military conflict. We're trained to think there must be a Good Guy and a Bad Guy, and that if a side isn't one then they're the other.

•

As far as the empire is concerned Palestinians have no more rights than whales dying from Navy sonar tests or wildlife in a prime military base location. Israel is a nuclear-armed imperial military outpost, and Palestinians, as far as the empire is concerned, are just in the way.

•

A nation which requires endless violence to maintain is not a real nation, anymore than a house which requires nonstop, round-the-clock construction work is a real house. If your house needed 24/7/365 construction work to prevent it from collapsing, you'd either move or come up with a radically different design plan.

•

I oppose warmongering against Venezuela and China and they say it's because I love communism.

I oppose warmongering against Iran and they say it's because I love theocracy.

I oppose warmongering against Russia and Syria and they say it's because I love autocracy.

Maybe I just oppose warmongering.

•

Once you realize that corporate power is the empire's real government, it becomes clear that corporate media is state media. It's just a tyrannical regime brainwashing its populace with propaganda, brutalizing protesters, and attacking anyone in the world who disobeys its dictates.

•

All arguments the US government makes against any "regime" it dislikes are completely invalidated by its alliance with Saudi Arabia *alone*, to say nothing of all the other tyrannical governments it's allied with.

•

Remember kids, if the US didn't torture journalists and whistleblowers, arm terrorists, kill children with starvation sanctions, wage endless wars, facilitate mass atrocities, repeatedly use nuclear weapons on civilian populations, circle the entire planet with hundreds of military bases and bully every nation on earth using military and economic force, an evil government might take over the world.

•

Foreign policy is the most consequential aspect of government behavior. The elite manipulators clearly understand this, while the rank-and-file public (even its well-informed oppositional members) usually don't. The trouble is that foreign policy is too big and too remote for most people to really grasp unless they're actively shown how their money and resources are stolen to pay for foreign military aggression. And the billionaire media are highly invested in not showing them this.

•

The only real "welfare queen" that's ever existed is the US military. Not even Reagan's most dementia-addled fantasies ever dreamed up a welfare moocher this minted.

•

There's no legitimate reason why nations can't just mind their own affairs and care for their own people. Having to read news every day about our government and its allies scheming to destroy nations which disobey them is severely disordered, and we should oppose it ferociously.

•

Arresting people for future crimes is called "pre-crime", and it's the stuff of dystopian horror fiction.

Violently dominating an entire planet because another country might hurt yours in the future is called "US foreign policy", and it's the stuff of mainstream news punditry.

•

US military expansionism is like the barb on a fish hook: no resistance from anyone sending the troops in, but massive resistance to pulling them back out.

•

Every dollar spent on keeping troops and military equipment outside a nation's borders was stolen from citizens who are trying to feed and house themselves.

•

Troops that are stationed outside a nation's borders are just glorified mall cops. They're not defending people, they're guarding resources and commercial interests. They're an army of Paul Blarts.

•

If a foreign government is authoritarian toward its own people and your government is authoritarian toward the entire world, then yours is the more authoritarian government.

If your attempts to fight tyranny help advance the planet-dominating agendas of the most powerful government on earth, then you're not fighting tyranny. You're facilitating it.

•

The first and foremost job of any US president is to serve as a decoy to draw the fire of all public scrutiny toward real power structures. Presidents are just narrative management ops the US empire uses to explain to the public why it is doing the things it was always going to do, like explaining what death is to children using puppets.

•

An honest war is as rare as an honest politician.

•

You know that person in your life who's always telling you what you should do despite the fact that their own life is a shambles and nobody likes them and they continuously make bad decisions for themselves? That's America on the world stage.

•

When it first rose to power with the Bush administration the neoconservative ideology of doing whatever it takes to ensure continued US unipolar hegemony was widely criticized. Now it's the bipartisan beltway consensus, and if you question it you're smeared as freakish and suspicious.

You never even hear the word neoconservative or neocon anymore in mainstream US discourse. That's not because it went away, it's because it became the normalized default mainstream worldview.

•

The way bombing creates extremism which is used to justify more bombing is one of the most psychopathically brilliant scams ever devised.

Step 1: Destroy nations and displace tens of millions of people.

Step 2: Wait for some of those people to hate you and want to fight back.

Step 3: Use their desire to fight back as justification to repeat Step 1.

•

Saudi Arabia is just an honest version of America. The tyranny is right out in the open, state censorship is straightforward instead of being outsourced to Silicon Valley, the oligarchs and the official government are the same people, they don't pretend their wars are humanitarian, and they just directly murder journalists they dislike instead of a using fake judicial system to do it.

•

The dumbest thing about believing foreign countries attacked American democracy is believing America has any democracy to attack.

Claiming a country attacked America's democracy is like claiming they attacked America's leprechauns.

•

Mentally replace every news headline about every US-targeted government with "Nation Insists On Its Own Financial, Economic, Resource and/or Military Sovereignty". You'll get a much more accurate picture of what's going on.

•

They don't prefer sanctions because they're more peaceful than all-out war, they prefer sanctions because they're easier to manufacture consent for. Start a war and you risk creating an antiwar movement. Kill the same number of people with sanctions and it'll barely be noticed.

•

Ask someone how much a dollar bill is worth and they'll tell you a dollar. Put a gun to their head and ask "Are you sure it's not worth 100 dollars?" and they'll say "Ah yes you're right, my mistake."

That's the economy under the US empire.

•

To oppose western interventionism is to put yourself in the uniquely absurd position of being branded an extremist lunatic and a foreign intelligence agent for objecting to something that is literally always disastrous.

•

If war propaganda stopped working and people realized what the imperial war machine is actually doing, it would immediately become impossible for the military to recruit.

"I joined the Army, Ma."

"You mean you're gonna kill kids for money? How am I supposed to tell people that??"

•

It's crazy how many self-described "anarchists" wind up advocating the same regime change agendas as the CIA and the US State Department. Like "Yeah I'm so anti-authoritarian I want the single most powerful authoritarian force on the planet to shore up even more control over the world."

•

Imagine someone coming up to you with a money jar saying "Excuse me, we're raising funds to build another military base in Somalia, would you care to make a donation?" No one would ever knowingly put money toward such an endeavor. Yet taxpayers do this unwittingly all the time.

•

The empire just keeps attempting coups until they stick. A kickboxer throws strikes in combinations with the understanding that most will miss or do minimal damage, but eventually one will connect and score the knockout blow. Imperialist coup agendas employ the same philosophy.

•

Things are so crazy because the reality of US unipolar hegemony's inevitable failure is crashing headlong into a world order which is built on the philosophy that US unipolar hegemony must be maintained at all cost.

•

The collapse of a nation will necessarily hurt the people who live there. The collapse of an unacknowledged globe-spanning empire won't necessarily hurt anybody.

•

The modern US imperial war machine kills more like a python than a tiger, placing less emphasis on the full-scale ground invasions of the Bush era and more on slowly suffocating the life out of targeted nations using sanctions, blockades, coups, psyops and CIA-backed uprisings.

•

Q: What is China?

A: China is a large Asiatic nation which westerners use as an emotional punching bag for their capitalism-induced rage, propaganda-induced confusion, and fears about the death of the US empire.

The nation that is circling the planet with hundreds of military bases and engaging in countless undeclared military operations around the world is the belligerent rogue nation. Everyone else is, at worst, acting in self-defense in response to this belligerence.

Governments using force to dominate the planet put every human being on a trajectory toward extinction via nuclear armageddon, and should be vehemently opposed. One government is the worst offender in this area, by a very, very, very wide margin. And it ain't freakin' China.

•

The main risk of cold war escalations is not that a government will decide to wage a nuclear war, it's that a nuke will be set off due to miscommunication or misfire amid heightening tensions (as nearly happened multiple times during the last cold war) and set MAD into motion.

This is what we're letting the morons in charge play with when they continue ramping up escalations against Russia and China. This isn't a fucking game. But we're letting them treat it like one. A bunch of children playing with armageddon weapons like fucking toys.

•

The position that detente should be sought with China and Russia is not a position that says their governments are wonderful, it's the position that the neoconservative ideology of US unipolar domination at all cost is not worth gambling the life of every terrestrial organism on.

•

The only reason people don't worry about cold war escalations against China and Russia like they do about hot wars with non-nuclear powers is because we got lucky in the last cold war. But that's all it was: sheer, dumb luck. No one was ever in control during that time. Not once.

•

Believing cold war is no big deal because nuclear war hasn't happened yet is the same as believing your game of Russian roulette is safe because the gun hasn't gone off yet.

•

Cornered animals are dangerous, especially ones with fangs and claws.

Dying empires are dangerous, especially ones with nuclear weapons.

•

I've been told countless times in a matter-of-fact tone that if the US didn't rule the world with unipolar hegemony then Beijing or Moscow would, but I've never once had someone back this claim up with a solid argument. There's simply no evidence that it's true.

The only thing we know would change if the US didn't rule the world is US-centralized power structures would lose the ability to sanction disobedient nations into oblivion and gin up support for coalition invasions. Everything else is just baseless conjecture assumed to be true, perhaps largely due to a projection of western evangelical and colonialist values upon a civilization that has never held those values. We assume they want what we want, and there's no evidence they do.

•

I talk about Iraq all the time because that's what everyone should be doing. It's never been addressed, never been resolved, yet the US war machine and its propaganda apparatus have marched on as though it never happened. It's a very large elephant in a very important room.

•

There's an implicit default assumption among the political/media class that US government agencies have earned back the trust they lost with Iraq, despite their having made no changes whatsoever to prevent another Iraq-like horror from reoccurring, or even so much as apologizing.

•

The Iraq invasion feels kind of like if your dad had stood up at the dinner table, cut off your sister's head in front of everyone, gone right back to eating and never suffered any consequences, and everyone just kind of forgot about it and carried on life like it never happened.

•

Most of the arguments you'll get from imperialists rest on the unspoken premise, "Let's pretend Iraq never happened."

•

Mentally replace the label "conspiracy theorist" with "Iraq rememberer".

•

All the corrupt mechanisms which led to the Iraq invasion are still in place and its consequences remain. It isn't something that happened in the past; it's happening now.

•

Supporting the Vietnam war was dumb. Supporting the Iraq invasion after being lied to about Vietnam was an order of magnitude dumber. Supporting any US war agendas after being lied to about Iraq is an order of magnitude even dumber than that.

•

No institutional changes were made to ensure that the evils of the Iraq invasion wouldn't be repeated. It's one of those big, glaring problems people just decided to pretend is resolved, like racism.

•

There are no war heroes, only war victims.

•

Always side against US imperialism. You'll always be right, you'll always look cool, you'll win every argument, and history will always vindicate you.

The Enemy

In Hollywood they make horror movies about a murderous psychopath running around slashing people, instead of making horror movies about the fact that murderous psychopaths rule our entire world this very moment.

•

The problem is that people without functioning empathy centers are willing to do anything to get power and are able to use narrative manipulation to obtain it. You can add as many individual details as you like, but around the world this is the primary obstacle to human thriving.

The main obstacle to humanity forming a collaborative relationship with each other and our ecosystem isn't because of human nature, it's because manipulative psychopaths keep working their way into power. Finding a way to deal with psychopathy would solve most of our problems.

•

Some people who learn a bit about what's really going on in the world start believing society's problems are being driven by otherworldly forces like reptilians or Satanism because it's more comfortable than grappling with the reality that our ills are very, very, very human.

•

Those pushing the continuation of wars, military expansionism, oligarchic corruption, exploitative neoliberalism, police militarization and Orwellian surveillance are the ones to oppose. Those pushing the opposite way are the ones to support. This perspective should be common sense and obvious to everyone, but it's been twisted by propaganda into a "fringe" opinion.

•

In a remotely sane world we'd regard people who promote endless war with the same revulsion as child rapists and serial killers.

•

The devious and depraved individuals who work in government agencies know that many great evils can be hidden behind people's entirely irrational tendency to dismiss their own suspicions with a "No, my government would never do something that devious and depraved!"

•

Exactly zero of the world's worst people are in prison.

•

Killing people and selling their organs will get you labeled a murderer. Selling the weapons used to kill the same number of people for the same amount of money in wars you actively lobbied for will get you labeled a job creator.

•

In days past leaders used to brutally slaughter their enemies in front of everyone and wear their body parts in case anyone got any funny ideas. Nowadays our leaders wear suits and ties, and they talk about freedom and democracy and family values, and they kill way more people.

•

Sociopaths know that hell is just a religious propaganda construct because they understand how narrative manipulation works. That's why they can create mass atrocities like Yemen and still sleep like babies.

•

The establishment pushes censorship for the same reason cult leaders and abusive partners work to isolate their victims: they don't want people sharing ideas and information with each other about their abuser, because that can lead to their escaping from the abuse.

•

Complaining about the existence of conspiracy theories is power-serving behavior. Instead, complain about the existence of government, corporate and financial secrecy which causes people to form speculative theories about what the powerful are up to behind that veil of opacity.

They concentrate all the power in these tiny little elitist circles, then say "You don't get to know what we're doing with all our power over here. Not only that, but you don't even get to talk to each other about what we might be doing, even though it could directly affect you."

How crazy is that? At the very least don't play along with them and police each other about it on top of that.

It's fine to discuss and debate the validity of individual theories (I do it all the time), but to complain about the fact that people form theories about possible conspiracies when we know for a fact that powerful people conspire is just infantile.

•

The very worst fringe conspiracy theories do far less damage than mainstream, establishment-promoted conspiracy theories.

•

Here's how politicians, media and government could eliminate conspiracy theories if they really wanted to:

- Stop lying all the time

- Stop killing people

- Stop promoting conspiracy theories

- Stop doing evil things in secret

- End government opacity

- Stop conspiring

•

Governments have obscenely well-funded intelligence agencies that are literally dedicated to orchestrating secret conspiracies around the world, but if you say they might be conspiring in some part of the world people call you crazy and weird.

•

Step 1: Legalize government secrecy so you can do evil things in secret.

Step 2: Use government secrecy to do many many evil things.

Step 3: Call anyone who says you do evil things in secret a crazy conspiracy theorist.

•

Saying the CIA is probably helping to foment uprisings against US-targeted governments, when that is literally openly their job, should not be a controversial take to have.

•

It should outrage everyone that our governments hide ugly secrets from us at all, let alone imprisoning and torturing people who try to help us find out about them.

We should be making our governments afraid to hide the truth from us. Instead our governments are making us afraid to try and learn the truth about them by brutally punishing anyone who tries. This is gravely disordered.

•

Want a healthy world? End secrecy for the powerful, break up all media and fully democratize it, and decriminalize psychedelics. Stop interfering in people's ability to clearly see what's going on in their world, in their nation and in themselves, and a healthy system will naturally arise.

•

The amount of power you have over other people should have an exactly inverse relationship to your right to privacy. The more power you have, the less secrecy you should be entitled to. Once your power reaches governmental level or its corporate/financial/political/media equivalent, that secrecy should be zero.

How crazy is it that we've allowed people to have power over us and also keep secrets from us? That by itself is bat shit insane. And then to let them shame us and punish us when we try to work out what they're up to behind that wall of opacity? Utter madness.

Nobody running any government should be allowed to have secrets. Yes, this will mean fewer people are interested in getting into government. That's as it should be. It shouldn't be enticing. It's meant to be a vocation, dedicated to public service. Public servants, private citizens. If you want privacy, then power should be made unappealing to you.

•

Murderous governments who deceive their citizenry are not entitled to any degree of secrecy whatsoever.

•

Rather than pretending to know exactly what type of revolutionary society would best lead to human thriving, you do have the option of just supporting the freeing up of all information and the end of all perception management and letting people figure it out for themselves.

End all government secrecy, end all political secrecy, end all corporate secrecy, end all Wall Street and financial secrecy, end all propaganda, give everyone equal media control, and just let people see clearly what the hell is actually truly going on in their world, and they'll naturally start using the power of their numbers to push for healthy changes in their own way. Let people see the actual truth of what's actually happening and stop using mass media to manipulate their understanding of the raw data and they can make informed decisions about what to do.

It's the authoritarian mind that thinks it knows exactly what's best for everyone. A respect for people's self-sovereignty really means you just want powerful manipulators to stop dicking around with everyone's understanding of the world so they can figure stuff out on their own.

Anyone with any interest in or access to power should be forbidden to keep secrets from the public. Like how crazy is it that DNC officials were allowed to conspire with each other in secret about how they were going to rule America in the first place? No, you don't get to do that. If you're part of a power structure, you have to show your work. Period.

If everyone could see what's really going on they'd create a world that is night-and-day different from the one we have now, and infinitely healthier. Which is why existing power structures pour so much effort into keeping people from seeing what's really going on.

I personally think that if people had all the information and weren't being manipulated by powerful interests they'd create a society that takes care of everyone and isn't driven by the pursuit of profit, but what the hell do I know? Give them clear vision and let them decide.

In any case, nobody's getting any revolutionary society of any kind as long as the powerful can control what information people have access to and manipulate the way they think and vote. There will be no revolution as long as people are manipulated into supporting the status quo.

.

Government says it needs secrecy to make war on its enemies effectively, and, curiously, the more secrecy we allow it the more wars and enemies it seems to have.

.

Government: We need to keep secrets from you.

Public: Why?

Government: We can't fight the wars against our enemies without secrecy.

Public: But we're not in any wars and we have no enemies.

Government: Yeah well it's hard to make them when you don't let us keep secrets from you.

.

A society is only as free as its most troublesome truth-teller.

.

Still mad at China's brutal authoritarian government for imprisoning Julian Assange after his journalism exposed Chinese war crimes.

•

Assange, verb. Use: To be assanged.

Meaning: when the nationless alliance of elites imprison a dissident by using their power to manipulate vagaries in the laws of their respective nations.

Eg "I have information on war crimes that I should leak but I don't want to be assanged."

•

Everyone I argue with online is basically just saying "Actually it's good for a small group of sociopaths to have all the power and we should definitely give them more."

•

The way politicians pretend to despise their opponents' depraved actions and then get all cuddly later proves they're not each other's enemy, they're yours.

•

The difference between the totalitarianism of dictatorships and the inverted totalitarianism of "free" societies is that in totalitarianism they allow one ideology which supports the status quo, while inverted totalitarianism allows two ideologies which support the status quo.

•

Placing yourself in the ideological center between two corporatist warmongering parties doesn't make you a centrist, it makes you a corporatist warmonger.

•

Things will remain fucked as long as "moderate" means standing between one warmongering political party that lets rich people screw you and another warmongering political party that lets rich people screw you.

•

Once you stop believing the fairy tale that there are two separate political parties in America – an evil and abusive one and a less evil and abusive one – you just see one big nasty dickhead telling you "Vote for my left-handed sock puppet or I'll beat you up with my right one."

What is the sane response to such a situation? Is it to placate this asshole and say "Oh no please sir don't beat me up, I'll play whatever game you want"? Or is it to stand up and say "How about no? How about you don't get to beat up anyone at all?"

•

America's two-party sock puppet show is always fake. Always. Buying into any part of it supports the whole fake show. "But the red puppet acts different from the blue puppet!" Yes. That's how puppet shows work. Characters act different. Cheering for either is endorsing the lie.

You can absolutely make the case that one of the puppets acts less reprehensibly than the other during the show. But the show always ends the same: everyone in the audience gets a punch in the mouth and has to give all their money to the military.

•

It's not that Democrats and Republicans are identical; if you look at each individually, you can see some differences. And that's how they get you. That's how the illusion is upheld. But if you zoom out a bit further, you see they're both used in conjunction to advance the same agendas.

There's a difference between Democrats and Republicans in the sense that there's a difference between the jab and the cross in boxing. The jab is often used to set up the more damaging cross, but they're both wielded by the same boxer, and they're both punching you in the face.

•

I invented an arcade game with a robotic boxing glove and two buttons. If you push the red button it punches you in the face, and if you push the blue one it punches you in the face while telling you the red one would've punched you a bit harder. No one played it for some reason.

•

Any political issue which doesn't directly threaten the interests of oligarchs and the military-industrial complex is incapable of delivering meaningful political change. It will be hijacked and used as a carrot or a stick by the two-headed one-party system to distract from anything that threatens existing power structures.

•

Know what's way more destructive than a dogshit president? A system which consistently ensures that voters always have to elect a dogshit president.

•

I can understand the logic of "vote for the lesser of two evils", I just can't understand why people only ever say that while pointing at one inseparably unified blob of evil.

•

Do you not think it odd that the single most important civic duty you're told you'll ever perform is always a vote for more war, more oligarchy, more authoritarianism, more ecocide, more exploitation and more plutocratic theft?

•

Mainstream Democrats and Republicans are violent extremists whose murderous ideology has caused orders of magnitude more death and destruction than any government-designated "terrorist" group.

•

Q: What is the Republican Party?

A: A narrative management operation which assures Americans of conservative sensibilities that the status quo is working fine.

Q: What is the Democratic Party?

A: A narrative management operation which assures Americans of liberal sensibilities that the status quo is working fine.

•

Democrats and Republicans are like male and female starfish; it's hard to tell them apart unless you're one of them.

•

We're hurtling toward multiple armageddon-level events on multiple fronts in the near term and people are still like "We can vote strategically and begin organizing a gradual progressive takeover in the Democratic Party beginning at the local level so that after 30-40 years…"

•

Establishment liberalism is just a bunch of people reassuring each other that you can change absolutely nothing and still feel self-righteous about it.

•

If mainstream liberals and conservatives applied the same standards and scrutiny to their own government that they apply to governments targeted by western imperialism, they'd be radical leftists.

•

Liberals hate leftists because leftists are a constant reminder that liberals aren't what they pretend to be.

•

Liberals hate leftists for the same reason you'd hate someone at a theater who kept yelling "These are all actors, none of this is real." Liberals are trying to enjoy a fictional performance about their side being heroic protagonists, and leftists keep disrupting the illusion.

•

Liberals are just rightists who understand how to market rightist policies.

·

Superhero comic writers often envisioned variations on an evil nerd inventing some powerful technology and trying to use it to take over the world. Their work turns out to have been prophetic, except the technology is more boring, and there are no superheroes to stop them.

·

A powerful institution made up a bunch of silly, arbitrary rules and sent out a bunch of deeply unconscious human beings to enforce those rules, so naturally it became very abusive. This is the story of the Catholic Church. It's also the story of the criminal justice system.

·

The ideologies of fundamentalist Christianity and Zionism have been used to manufacture consent for the movement of far more military firepower than Islam ever has. All religions are ultimately toxic, but only idiots pretend Islam occupies a uniquely violent position among them.

Anyone who's ever escaped from a relationship with a sociopath can see these "We stand with the people of Nation X in rising up against their government" scripts for the imperialist manipulations they are. It's amazing how many of the people with deep understandings of manipulation are survivors of this type of abuse.

•

Just because there are powerful people conspiring to do terrible things does not mean they will succeed. They are not wise, they are not particularly smart, and they fail frequently. Don't make gods of these assholes.

A lot of people think of the oligarchs like Greek deities maneuvering chess pieces from on high at Mount Olympus with total control over the affairs of mortals. In reality they're just sociopaths who don't understand normal humans all that well, and their agendas often faceplant. Don't fall into the trap of believing every minute detail of everything that happens is controlled by nigh-omnipotent manipulators. They're just clever primates who know a few tricks; they don't really understand healthy humans, and we constantly move in ways they didn't predict.

Humanity has so very, very much more potential than even most healthy humans understand, let alone sociopaths with no deep insight into the human condition. Things are shifting, and the sociopaths will be the very last ones to know it. They have no idea what's coming.

•

May empathy become the new currency. May humanity become so compassionate and empathy-driven that severe mental illness is no big deal since you'll get all the help you need, but being psychopathic or sociopathic is a severe handicap in which the inability to empathize sticks out to everyone like a sore thumb.

There's Only One News Story, Repeating Over And Over Again

Doing daily commentary on world power dynamics feels a lot like staring up at the sky watching clouds. Sometimes you see a three-legged pony up there, sometimes a gargoyle, sometimes a laughing baby, but really you're only ever watching tiny water droplets being moved around by atmospheric winds. They can take on any number of different shapes, but no matter how long you lay there staring up at them you're really only ever seeing one dynamic play out with different appearances from moment to moment.

The daily news is very much the same, except most consumers of news media aren't aware that they're watching clouds. They really do think they're looking at a three-legged pony, a gargoyle, a laughing baby.

"Ooh, there's a doggy!" they squeal and clap their hands. "Ooh! Ooh now it's a kitty cat!"

They don't see the real underlying dynamics, they just see the forms those dynamics are taking from moment to moment. They don't see the water droplets being moved around by the breeze, they just see the shapes.

Just as clouds are always water droplets in the air no matter what shapes they take, news stories are only ever one dynamic playing out with different appearances.

There is only ever one news story on any given day, and it is always the same news story: wealthy and powerful people seek more wealth and power, and narratives are spun to advance these agendas.

That's it. That's all you're ever seeing when you read the news. There are sports scores and the occasional celebrity death mixed in for entertainment, but when it comes to major political and governmental events you're only ever seeing the effects of wealthy and powerful people working to obtain more wealth and power and narratives being spun to promote these agendas.

Today it's the Democratic Party killing the $15 minimum wage, protests in Haiti, US electoral shenanigans in Ecuador, bombings and sanctions on Syria, China bad, Russia bad. Appearances which taken individually at first glance look like breaking news stories, but when examined closely and integrated into the big picture are actually the exact same dynamics that were playing out yesterday with slightly different shapes. Tomorrow those same dynamics will play out again in different appearances. The shapes are different, but it's always water droplets in the air.

It's the exact same news story playing out over and over and over again, day after day after day. Alarm clock goes off at 6 a.m., Sonny and Cher sing "I Got You Babe", and Bill Murray wakes up to Groundhog Day once again.

"Well it looks like Jibby Jorpson is set to be the new leader, somehow staving off an early challenge from the popular socialist candidate," reports the news man. "In other news, the ostensibly left-wing party will be unable to help the working class due to bliff blaff bloffa reasons, a dangerous dictator in a crucial geostrategic region urgently needs to be removed from power because widdle diddle doodad, and coming up: do we need more internet censorship to prevent wakka dakka dingdong?"

Next morning. Alarm clock. "I Got You Babe", Bill Murray, Groundhog Day again.

"Well it looks like Miggy Morpson is set to be the the the new leader, somehow staving off an early challenge from the popular socialist candidate," reports the news man. "In other news, the ostensibly left-wing party will be unable to help the working class due to wing wang wappa reasons, a dangerous dictator in a crucial geostrategic region urgently needs to be removed from power because kooka kakka keeka, and coming up: do we need more internet censorship to prevent yope yap yimmy?"

Over and over and over again. And over and over and over. The excuses change, the narrative spin changes, the component parts of the agendas change, but it's only ever the same one story: wealthy and powerful people seek more wealth and power, and narratives are spun to advance these agendas.

Once you see the clouds as clouds, you never again get confused about what those shapes in the sky really are. You see different iterations of the exact same dynamic where you used to see individual breaking news stories.

When you have this insight and realize it's always the same story playing out over and over again, there's a common temptation to give in to despair and bitterness. Maybe you keep fighting, but you do it with a bored, jaded and entirely uninspired mentality.

It doesn't need to be this way though. Just because the fight isn't happening the way you used to imagine doesn't mean it's hopeless or tedious, it just means you need to look at it differently. You don't have a 50-fight career against 50 different opponents who you fought for 10 rounds each, you have a one-fight career against a single opponent who you've been fighting for 500 rounds.

Just because the fight is longer than you once thought and the opponent much more resilient than you once thought doesn't mean that one long fight is without end, or that it is unwinnable. It just means it looks different than it used to. It was ponies and doggies, now it's clouds. You still bite down on your mouthpiece and throw leather with all your strength.

But it's important to do it with focus on the whole. When we oppose ruling power structures and the narratives that they are using to advance their agendas, it's important to also zoom out and point to their place in the whole. It benefits no one to treat any of the manifestations of the recurring one news story as separate from all the other arrangements: you've got to tie it in to the greater dynamics of empire and oligarchy at every opportunity. Otherwise you're just feeding into the illusion of doggies and kitties in the sky.

That's all we're ever doing here: trying to point to the recurring Groundhog Day story over and over again from as many different angles as possible to help people see the clouds. We can use individual news stories as illustrations to show people the bigger picture of what's really going on, but really all we're ever doing is helping them see it all as water droplets arranging in different shapes from day to day.

Help enough people see the big picture, and the fight is as good as won. Then, and only then, does Bill Murray awaken to a new day.

Learning To Pierce Through The Fog Of Manipulation

Beginning sincere research into what's really going on with our world behind the veils of propaganda and government secrecy reveals many experts with a profound understanding of our actual circumstances. Further research reveals that no, actually they're all mostly faking it.

The first step to forming a solid understanding of the world is dispensing with the belief that others have a solid understanding of the world. Our society is full of prominent people who act like they know what's going on, and they're mostly bullshitting. Follow no one and trust only your own inner sensemaker; everyone else is lost too.

You can have the feeling that you totally know what's true or you can have a humble devotion to trying to learn the truth as best you can from moment to moment. You can't have both.

Gaining an understanding of what's going on in the world is a skill, just like any other. Like any other skill you kinda suck at it at first, then you get better with practice. The trick is to keep improving; never stop, either out of frustration or because you think you're done.

Be patient and compassionate with yourself when it comes to developing your narrative navigating skills. If you learn you've been wrong about something, just take in the new information, adjust appropriately, and keep plugging away. Don't expect to have mastered this thing before you've had time to master it.

•

Ignore all the narratives about why things need to be as they are, and you simply see things as they are: resources disappearing from the hands of the many into the hands of the few, weapons of war circling the globe, imprisonment, surveillance and censorship. That's what's real.

•

Any attempt to understand the world which fails to take into account the fact that extremely powerful people are pouring massive amounts of money and resources into manipulating your understanding of the world will necessarily result in a distorted worldview.

The problems our species now faces are the result of elite sociopathic manipulators using media to exploit human cognitive glitches which enable them to control the fate of the whole. Any analysis of our plight which doesn't account for this is a flawed, power-serving analysis.

•

Be humble and open enough to know that you can be fooled. Your cognitive wiring is susceptible to the same hacks as everyone else, and manipulators of all sorts are always looking to exploit those vulnerabilities.

It's not shameful to be deceived, it's shameful to deceive people. Don't let shame and cognitive dissonance keep you compartmentalized away from considering the possibility that you've been duped in some way.

•

Familiarize yourself with cognitive biases, the glitches in human cognition which cause us to perceive things in a way that is not rational. Humans have an annoying tendency to seek out cognitive ease in their information-gathering and avoid cognitive dissonance, rather than seeking out what's true regardless of whether it brings us cognitive ease or dissonance.

This means we tend to choose what we believe based on whether believing it is psychologically comfortable, rather than whether it's solidly backed by facts and evidence. This is a weakness in our cognitive wiring, and manipulators can and do exploit it constantly. And, again, be humble enough to know that this means you.

•

Trust your own understanding above anyone else's. It might not be perfect, but it's a damn sight better than letting your understanding be controlled by narrative managers and dopey partisan groupthink, or by literally anyone else in a narrative landscape that is saturated with propaganda and manipulation. You won't get everything right, but betting on your own understanding is the very safest bet on the table.

It can be intimidating to stand alone and sort out the true from the false by yourself on an instance-by-instance basis, but the alternative is giving someone else authority over your understanding of the world. Abdicating your responsibility to come to a clear understanding of what's going on in your world is a shameful, cowardly thing to do. Be brave enough to insist that you are right until such time as you yourself come to your own understanding that you were wrong.

People, generally speaking, are pretty unconscious. Until that changes, you can't rely on the collective for a clear idea of what matters and what's going on in the world. The group mind lacks both wisdom and intelligence. This is true of literally all groups and factions.

You've got to figure it out on your own—take responsibility for your understanding. You can't rely on anyone else to do it for you, and you can't look to what your ideological faction is excited about today for any clues. You'll be misled. Focus on honing your inner sense maker.

•

Understand that propaganda is the single most overlooked and under-appreciated aspect of our society, and that the science of mass-scale manipulation has been in research and development for a very long time. Think about how many military advancements have been made in the last hundred years, then recall again that it was a bit over a century ago that the US government first recruited Edward Bernays in its war effort to refine the science of modern propaganda.

Everyone's constantly talking about what's wrong with the world, but hardly any of those discussions are centered around the fact that the public has been manipulated into supporting the creation and continuation of those problems by mass media propaganda. The fact that powerful people are constantly manipulating the way we think, act and vote should be at the forefront of everyone's awareness, not relegated to occasional discussions in fringe circles.

•

Understand that western mass media propaganda rarely consists of full, outright lies. At most, such outlets will credulously publish the things that are told to them by government agencies which lie all the time. More often, the deception comes in the form of distortions, half-truths, and omissions. Pay more attention to discrepancies in things that are covered versus things that aren't, and to what they're not saying.

•

Put effort into developing a good news-sense, a sense for what's newsworthy and what's not. This takes time and practice, but it lets you see which newsworthy stories are going unreported by the mass media and which non-stories are being overblown to shape an establishment-friendly narrative. When you've got that nailed down, you'll notice "Why are they acting like this is a news story?" and "Why is nobody reporting this??" stories all the time.

•

Find reliable news reporters who have a good sense for navigating the narrative matrix, and keep track of them to orient yourself and stay on top of what's going on. Use individual reporters, not outlets; no outlet is 100 percent solid, but some reporters are pretty close on some specific subjects.

•

Don't let paranoia be your primary or only tool for navigating the narrative matrix. Some people's only means of understanding the world is to become intensely suspicious of everything and everyone, which is about as useful as a compass which tells you that every direction is north. Spend time in conspiracy and media criticism circles and you'll run into many such people.

Rejecting everything as false leaves you with nothing as true. Find positive tools for learning what's true.

•

Hold your worldview loosely enough that you can change it at any time in the light of new information, but not so loosely that it can be slapped out of your head by someone telling you what to think in a confident, authoritative tone. As Carl Sagan once said, "It pays to keep an open mind, but not so open your brains fall out."

•

Speaking of confident, authoritative tones, be suspicious of confident, authoritative tones. It's amazing how much traction people can get with a narrative just by posturing as though they know that what they're saying is true, whether they're an MSNBC pundit or a popular conspiracy Youtuber.

So many people are just plain faking it, because it works. You run into this all the time in debates on online political forums; people come at you with a supremely confident posture, but if you push them to present their knowledge on the subject and the strength of their arguments, there's not actually anything there. They're just accustomed to people assuming they know what they're talking about and leaving their claims unchallenged, and it completely throws them off when someone doesn't buy their feigned confidence schtick.

There'd be a lot less confusion in political discourse if people really intuitively understood that there is no correlation between how confidently someone says something and how true it is.

•

Be acutely aware that the only reason the status quo is accepted as "normal", and its defenders regarded as "moderate", is because vast fortunes are poured into making it seem that way. If we could see the status quo of this world with fresh eyes, we'd scream in horror.

•

Remain always aware of this simple dynamic: the people who become billionaires are generally the ones who are sociopathic enough to do whatever it takes to get ahead. This class has been able to buy up near-total narrative control via media ownership/influence, corporate lobbying, think tank funding, and campaign finance, and are thus able to manipulate the public into consenting to agendas which benefit nobody but plutocrats and their lackeys. This explains pretty much every major problem that we are facing right now.

•

Understand that war is the glue which holds the US-centralized empire together. Without the carrot of military/economic alliance and the stick of military/economic violence, the US-centralized empire would cease to exist.

This is why war propaganda is constant and sometimes so forced that glaring plot holes become exposed; it's so important that they need to force it through, even if they can't get the narrative matrix around it constructed just right.

If they ceased manufacturing consent for the empire's relentless warmongering, people would lose all trust in government and media institutions, and those institutions would lose the ability to propagandize the public effectively. Without the ability to propagandize the public effectively, our rulers cannot rule.

•

Know that the truth has no political party, and neither do the social engineers. All political parties are used to manipulate the masses in various ways, and nuggets of truth can and do emerge from any of them. Thinking along partisan lines is guaranteed to give you a distorted view. Ignore the imaginary lines between the parties. You may be certain that your rulers do.

•

Understand that nations are pure narrative constructs; they only exist to the extent that people agree to pretend that they do. The narrative managers know this, and they exploit the fact that most of us don't.

Take Julian Assange for example: he was pried out of the embassy and imprisoned by an extremely obvious collaboration between the US, UK, Sweden, Ecuador, and Australia, yet they each pretended that they were acting as separate, sovereign nations completely independently of one another. Sweden pretended it was deeply concerned about rape allegations, the UK pretended it was deeply concerned about a bail violation, Ecuador pretended it was deeply concerned about skateboarding and embassy cat hygiene, the US pretended it was deeply concerned about the particulars of the way Assange helped Chelsea Manning cover her tracks, Australia pretended it was too deeply concerned about honoring the sovereign affairs of these other countries to intervene on behalf of its citizen, and it all converged in a way that just so happened to look exactly the same as imprisoning a journalist for publishing facts.

You see this same dynamic constantly, whether it's with military interventions, trade deals, or narrative-shaping campaigns against non-aligned governments.

•

Remember that when it comes to foreign policy, the neocons are always wrong. They've been so remarkably consistent in this for so long that whenever there's a question about any narrative involving hostilities between the US-centralized power alliance and any other nation, you can just look at what Bill Kristol, Max Boot and John Bolton are saying about it and believe the exact opposite. They're actually a very helpful navigation tool in this way.

•

Notice how the manipulators like to split the population in two and then get them arguing over how they should serve the establishment. Arguing over whether it's better to vote Democrat or Republican, arguing over whether it's better to increase hostilities with Iran and Venezuela or with Syria and Russia, over whether you should support the US president or the FBI, arguing over how internet censorship should happen and whom should be censored rather than if censorship should happen in the first place.

The longer they can keep us arguing over the best way to lick the imperial boot, the longer they keep us from talking about whether we want to lick it at all.

•

Whenever the political/media class begin declaring that some dastardly deed has been committed which requires immediate military action, your default assumption should be that they're lying, because they've got an extensively documented history of doing so. After lying so consistently about such things so many times, the burden of proof is always on the western power structures who are making the claim, and that burden requires mountains of independently verifiable evidence to be met.

If a known compulsive liar who has deceived you many times in the past told you it was very, very important that you go and murder your neighbor, but he couldn't show you the evidence proving his claim, would you take him at his word and get your gun? No? Then don't trust western power structures when they tell you something happened requiring military action.

•

Dismiss all Latest Official Bad Guy narratives. The only ones who benefit from you hating a foreign government are the powerful people who are targeting that government and seeking to manufacture support for future actions against it. Don't be a dupe, and don't be a pro bono CIA propagandist. Just look at the objective, independently verifiable information.

•

Watch out for appeals to emotion. It's much easier to manipulate someone by appealing to their feely bits rather than their capacity for rational analysis, which is why any time they want to manufacture support for military interventionism you see pictures of dead children on news screens everywhere rather than a logical argument for the advantages of using military violence based on a thorough presentation of facts and evidence.

You see the same strategy used in the guilt trips they lay on third-party voters; it's all emotional hyperbole that crumbles under any fact-based analysis, but they use it because it works. They go after your heart strings to circumvent your head.

•

Make a practice of asking "Who benefits from this narrative I'm being sold?" and "Who benefits from this belief I have?" Who benefits from your hating China or the Latest Official Bad Guy? Who benefits from the belief that the status quo is acceptable? Keep asking this about the narratives coming to you, and about the beliefs you already hold in your head.

•

Pay attention to how much propaganda goes into maintaining the propaganda machine itself. This is done this because propaganda is just that central to the maintenance of dominant power structures. Much effort is spent building trust in establishment narrative management outlets while sowing distrust in sources of dissent. You'll see entire propaganda campaigns built around accomplishing solely this.

•

Understand that truth doesn't generally move in a way that is pleasing to the ego, i.e. in a way Hollywood scripts are written to appeal to. Any narrative that points to a Hollywood ending where the bad guy gets karate kicked into lava and the hero gets the girl is manufactured.

Ever since 2016 it's become the norm for America's two mainstream political factions to be constantly screaming that an earth-shattering scandalous revelation is about to bring about the collapse of the other party any minute now, and it just never happens, and it never will. Reality doesn't move that way.

•

Be acutely aware that sociopaths exist. There are people who, to varying degrees, do not care what happens to others, and these are the types of people who will use manipulation to get their way whenever it serves them. If you don't care about truth or other people beyond the extent to which you can use them, then there's no disincentive to manipulating.

•

Be aware of projection, and be aware of the fact that it cuts both ways: unhealthy people tend to project their wickedness onto others, while healthy people tend to project their goodness. Don't let your goodness trick you into thinking there aren't monsters who will deceive and manipulate you, and don't let sociopaths project their own sinister motives onto you by telling you how rotten you are. This mixes a lot of good people up, especially in their personal lives. Not everyone is good, and not everyone is truthful. See this clearly.

•

Watch people's behavior and ignore the stories they tell about their behavior. This applies to people in your life, to politicians, and to governments. Narratives can be easily manipulated and distorted in many different ways, while behavior itself, when examined with as much objectivity as possible, cannot be. Pay attention to behavior in this way and eventually you'll start noticing a large gap between what some people's actions say and what their words say. Those people are the manipulators. Distrust them.

•

Be suspicious of people who keep telling you what they are and how they are, because they're trying to manipulate your narrative about them. Be doubly suspicious of people who keep telling you what you are and how you are, because they're trying to manipulate your narrative about you.

•

Learn to see how trust and sympathy are used by manipulators to trick people into subscribing to their narratives about what's going on. Every manipulator uses trust and/or sympathy as a primer for their manipulations, because if you don't have trust or sympathy for them, you're not going to mentally subscribe to their stories.

This is true of mass media outlets, it's true of State Department press releases which implore you to have sympathy for the people of Nation X, and it's true of family members and coworkers. Once you've spotted a manipulator, your task is to kill off all of your sympathy for them and your trust in them, no matter how hard they start playing the victim to suck you back in.

•

Be suspicious of anyone who refuses to articulate themselves clearly. Word salading is a tactic notoriously used by abusive narcissists, because it keeps the victim confused and unable to figure out what's going on. If they can't get a clear handle on what the manipulative abuser is saying, they can't form their own solid position in relation to it, and the abuser knows this. Insist on lucid communication, and if it's refused to you, remove trust and sympathy. Apply this to people in your life, to government officials, and to online psyops like QAnon.

•

Be suspicious of those who excessively advocate civility, rules and politeness. Manipulators thrive on rules and civility, because they know how to manipulate them. Someone who's willing to color outside the lines and get angry at someone noxious even when they're acting within the rules makes a manipulator very uncomfortable.

Often times those telling you to calm down and behave yourself when you are rightfully upset are manipulators who have a vested interest in getting you to adhere to the rules set they've learned to operate within.

•

Be relentlessly honest with yourself about your own inner narratives and the various ways you engage in manipulation. You can't navigate your way through the narrative matrix if you aren't clear on your own role in it. Look inside and consciously take an inventory.

•

Try to view the world with fresh eyes rather than with your tired old grown-up eyes which have taught you to see all this as normal. Hold an image in your mind of what a perfectly healthy and harmonious world would look like; the sharp contrast between this image and the world we have now allows you see through the campaign of the propagandists to normalize things like war, poverty, ecocide, and impotent electoral systems which keep seeing the same government behavior regardless of who people vote for. None of this is normal.

•

Meditation, mindfulness, self-inquiry and other practices are powerful tools which can help you understand your own inner processes, which in turn helps you understand how manipulators can manipulate you, and how they manipulate others.

Just be sure that you are using them for this purpose, not for escapism as most "spiritual" types do. You're trying to become fully aware of what makes you tick mentally, emotionally and energetically; you're not trying to become some vapid spiritual bliss bunny. The goal isn't to feel better, the goal is to get better at feeling. Better at consciously experiencing your own inner world.

•

Learn the art of perceiving life without the perceptual filter of narrative. Mentally "mute" the narrative soundtrack and watch where all the resources are going, where the weapons are moving to and coming from, who's being killed and imprisoned etc, to get a clear picture of what's going on in the world.

Almost everything in the news is empty/irrelevant narrative. The only relevant information is where the money is moving, where the resources are moving, where the weapons are moving, and where the people are moving. Everything else is narrative meant to justify, manipulate or distract from those movements.

•

The maneuverings of establishment power structures are always made to protect the power they already have and/or to try and obtain more. It's never anything more exotic or otherworldly than that: the mundane, primitive drive to try and control as many other humans as possible.

•

The greatest asset of the propagandists is your belief that you haven't been propagandized.

•

If you ever want to understand what the US power alliance is doing on the world stage, just think about what it would need to do in order to ensure continual unipolar global domination, then ignore all the excuses it makes up for doing those exact things.

There's basically only ever one international news story: "Globe-spanning US-centralized empire tries to grow larger by absorbing more countries, and those countries resist." All news about global politics is just different manifestations of that one story, seen from different angles.

•

Most adults are aware that their government has lied about things. It's only propaganda, and the human tendency to compartmentalize away from uncomfortable facts, which keeps them from connecting that dot to the possibility that their government is lying to them *currently*.

•

Not everything the US establishment does is a considered strategic maneuver; often it's just the frantic, confused flailings of a dying empire. The neocons sold the idea of a last-ditch gambit to shore up unipolarity, and it failed. And now it's all unraveling in some crazy ways.

•

If you find yourself cheering for the same "people's uprising" in a foreign nation that the US State Department is also loudly cheering for, it's because you've been propagandized. Please revise your media consumption habits and critical thinking skills accordingly.

•

The powerful use ideologies as tools to manipulate mainstream narratives to their advantage. Religious fundamentalism, Zionism, racism, anti-racism, liberalism, conservatism; they'll use anything they can. Pay less attention to the tools and more to what they're being used for.

•

There's little or no relation between what the mass media direct people to care about and what actually matters. If you get all worked up about the Hot Topic of the Day like everyone else you're usually just clapping along with a plutocratic puppet show made for stunted children.

•

Most military issues are a lot more simple and clear-cut than most "experts" claim, because those experts are paid to narrative manage military agendas. Pundits who babble about the "complexities of the Middle East" are just obfuscating the simple fact that we shouldn't be there.

•

When both mainstream parties exist to deceive you, it's impossible to inform yourself using mainstream partisan narratives without being deceived. They're both worldviews that are deliberately designed to distort your perception.

•

The words "I don't support war but" are always followed by a talking point that is being circulated to manufacture support for acts of war.

•

It's weird how parents and teachers tell kids that fighting is always wrong no matter who started it when we all know damn well the question of who started it is of immense importance in any real conflict.

•

All major world religions have spent centuries inseparably interlaced with powerful governments. This means they are all interlaced with ancient proto-propaganda from those governments. All that stuff glorifying meekness, obedience and poverty is made-up, power-serving hogwash.

•

If you want to understand how narrative management works in the world, pay attention to how it plays out in your own life. What are some popular narratives within your family, perhaps about one of your family members, that don't reflect reality? What subjects are off limits in your immediate or extended family, and why? Who do you know that repeatedly spins narratives about the kind of person they are, or the kind of person you are?

Most of us have at least one strong narrative manipulator in our circle somewhere; family, friends, work, etc. You can spot them by how much energy they pour into manufacturing a consensus about someone in their circle, including themselves; working to spin narratives about themselves that make them look good, or narratives about someone else to make them look bad.

Spot the manipulators in your own life and watch their patterns, then look out to the world and compare those patterns to what you see with government and media. You'll see the exact same patterns on a macro scale. Manipulation takes the same form whether small-scale or large.

•

Make and keep these two promises to any manipulator in your life and they'll lose all power over you forever:

"I promise you that I will never again believe anything you tell me about yourself."

"I promise you that I will never again believe anything you tell me about me."

•

A lot of people seem to think understanding what's really going on in the world just means cramming a bunch of information into your head. Information is key, but it's only part of it. Wisdom and inner clarity are also needed, and far too many neglect cultivating that aspect.

●

The world isn't happening the way most people think it is happening. Maturity is learning and understanding the multifaceted, multi-leveled ways in which this is the case.

Collective Revolution

It's not that you can't beat the machine, it's that you can't beat the machine using the tools the machine has offered you.

·

Things won't change for the better unless the people use the power of their numbers to force that change.

That won't happen as long as people are propagandized.

People will remain propagandized until something fundamentally shifts in their collective relationship with narrative.

I talk about fighting establishment narrative control a lot, not because it's the best way to change things, but because it's the *only* way. The public will never, ever use the power of their numbers to change things so long as they're being successfully propagandized not to.

·

If we're honest with ourselves, electoral politics has failed and we need a revolution.

If we're really honest with ourselves, revolution will fail until propaganda is eliminated.

If we're really really honest with ourselves, everything will fail without a mass-scale awakening.

•

If we make it out of this mess, it won't be because anyone's ideology won out over the others, it will be because we fundamentally changed the way we function as a species. It will be because we completely transformed our relationship with abstract thought and mental narrative.

•

Humanity in and of itself is not the problem. The problem is that we sometimes produce humans whose brains lack functioning empathy centers, who use the advantage this gives them over the rest of us in their relationship with mental narrative to manipulate us to get things they want.

•

What's required for a healthy world is not human extinction or a mass die-off, but a change in our collective relationship with mental narrative, where we use thought as a useful tool instead of the center of all our interest and attention. This change has always been possible.

People have been writing about the potential in humanity to awaken from the illusory nature of the mind and see reality clearly for thousands of years. What's different now is (A) our newfound ability to share information and (B) the fact that we are now at evolve-or-die time. And we'll either make that jump or we won't. But we absolutely do have the ability and the freedom to transcend our unhealthy relationship with mental narrative which gives sociopaths the ability to manipulate us toward our collective doom.

•

The most revolutionary thing you can do is use your creativity to find ways of helping people see the insanity of the status quo with fresh eyes. Punching holes in the manufactured normality so that people can see beyond the bullshit they've all gotten used to and really grok just how ugly and disgusting things have gotten will do infinitely more damage to the empire than just listing facts and figures and talking about how things ought to be.

•

To awaken from the establishment propaganda matrix is extremely uncomfortable, because the status quo becomes intolerable. This is a good thing. It means if you can help someone else awaken they'll experience the same discomfort, which will drive them to awaken others, and so on.

•

They can't arrest us all, and they can't kill us all. They know it and we know it. That's the whole reason for all the propaganda, censorship and surveillance. And no amount of propaganda, censorship and surveillance will be enough when it's time to force real change.

•

Hoping that a critical mass of people rise up and force change, despite being aggressively propagandized not to, is hoping for a miracle. The unspoken part of our plan is always "And then hopefully we'll just spontaneously start waking up." They talk about organizing and grassroots activism, but these plans always include an unacknowledged x-factor in which people suddenly begin working against the interests of establishment power structures for some miraculous reason and begin turning this ship around.

Revolutionary thought is an act of faith. If we're honest with ourselves, as a group we're a fair bit less atheistic than we pretend to be.

And yet, I maintain that this faith is entirely reasonable. I believe we do have the seeds of a miracle planted deep within us. I've seen too much not to.

•

I am optimistic that we'll be okay because I know that humanity has untapped potential in areas within ourselves that we've barely even begun discussing, much less researching. The manipulators only understand thoughts and language, and there's so much more to us than that.

We have the potential to break our conditioning patterns, which is huge because our conditioning patterns are what brought us to this point. Every species eventually hits a point where it either evolves or dies, and I already see signs of mass scale unpatterning. We can make it.

Long-established patterns are now being disrupted on a mass scale, creating lots of space to form new ones. Where there used to be a solid brick wall, there are now many gaps with plenty of space to shine light through. Make sure you take advantage of this.

•

We're looking at a life-or-death existential struggle here, both for the establishment and for the people. The difference is establishment lackeys stand to lose status and cocktail party invites, while the people stand to lose their lives. Who do you reckon has more to fight for?

•

Humanity has trolled itself into an evolve-or-die predicament. We've placed ourselves in check on the chessboard just right so that the only way to avoid checkmate is to collectively awaken from egoic consciousness. There's something inside us that is moving quite cleverly.

•

The most distinctive feature of the last few years has been expanding consciousness. Expanding consciousness of media corruption, of political corruption, of government corruption, of the abuse of immigrants, of police militarization, of unhealed racial wounds, etc.

It's encouraging. You can't fix something you haven't made conscious. This is true of our own unresolved psychological issues, and it's true of our unresolved collective issues as well. The first step toward a healthy world is expanded consciousness.

This is why increasing government opacity, internet censorship, and the war on journalism are so dangerous. Corruption and abuse thrive in darkness, and corrupt abusers want to keep that darkness intact. They want to keep things as unconscious as possible.

•

The more I learn about the human condition, the clearer it becomes that the principles of individual healing apply to collective healing as well. I have learned that an individual can experience a sudden, drastic shift in consciousness. I see no reason the collective can't also.

•

If we win this thing it won't be because conspiracy analysts showed everyone a bunch of complex financial connections or because Marxists put a bunch of theory in everyone's heads, it will be because clear, simple pointing helped everyone wake up to something that was already right in front of them.

This fight isn't a game of addition, it's a game of subtraction. You're not trying to get the mainstream rank-and-file public to understand a bunch of complicated new information, you're trying to remove the blindfold so they can see something for themselves that they kind of already suspected was the case.

Cripple public trust in the establishment narrative control apparatus and you remove the only obstacle that's been stopping the people from using the power of their numbers to force real change. They don't need anything new, they need to exorcise the lies that have blinded them and stop trusting in the words of liars.

•

Speak the truth and be loud about it. Choosing not to speak out is just making that much more space for the manipulative liars who are shouting above everyone as they drive our world into disaster, and you are much smarter, wiser, and more qualified to speak than they are.

No matter how unqualified you might feel to speak, you are infinitely more qualified than the loudest voices in our society who normalize and defend our murderous, oppressive, exploitative status quo using lies and manipulation. Speak even louder and more confidently than them.

•

You are also infinitely more qualified to report the news than all the scumbags in the mass media who are paid by billionaires to parrot government lies. I mean that 100 percent literally. If you're not being paid by the wealthy to lie to the public, you are more qualified to report the news than those who are. Doesn't matter if all you have is a smartphone and a Twitter account; you are set up to be a better news reporter than them.

You know all that space mass media reporters take up in society's awareness proclaiming what's true and what's going on in the world? That's your space. They usurped it. Take it back from them. The MSM have betrayed humanity to an unforgivable extent. We must become the media. Even a teenager making a sloppy, amateurish first-time Youtube video about current events is superior to a mass media talking head who's paid to lie. Be the press.

•

It is true that social media platforms are run by oligarchs and depraved government agencies. It is also true that ideas and information are moving vastly faster than they used to, in a way establishment power structures can't really keep up with. Denying either of these is dumb.

People who say "Twitter isn't real life" really mean "Twitter isn't mainstream life". It's the innovators, early adopters, influencers, cool hunters. Obviously this bleeds into the mainstream. It's what university culture used to be, only far more populist and democratic, and much faster.

Mainstream media has always prevented enlightened ideas from ever moving at the speed of print or broadcast media, which means until social media they mostly moved at the speed of university papers and books. They took literally years to circulate. The speed jumped from that to instantaneous. To think this isn't having an impact on our collective consciousness is demented. Our species has literally never looked anything like this. We're now like a giant planetary brain in which each of the billions of internet-connected humans is a neuron. This can't not change us.

Obviously establishment power structures are working to bring this unprecedented movement of ideas and information under tight control, but there's only so much control you can exert over a force this big. Past a certain point it's like trying to wrestle a tornado. We're moving.

•

People ask me "Well, what should we do? How do we fix this thing?" And of course my only possible answer is, "Do what I'm doing! Or your version of it." Of course I'm doing the thing I think we should do to solve the problems of our species. Why would I be doing anything else?

•

The only reason anything ever changes for the better is because of an expansion of consciousness. Awareness spreads of the evils of slavery, the injustice of racial and sexual inequality etc, and then things change. In each case there are forces promoting that expansion, and forces opposing it.

That's all we're ever fighting to accomplish here: expanding awareness in individuals and in the collective beyond the barriers of propaganda and status quo normalization to carry the true nature of important issues from unconsciousness to consciousness.

People don't change their behavior patterns because they're told to or because they spontaneously decide to, they do it when the unconscious forces which have been compelling those behavior patterns move into consciousness (which is why inner work is so important for recovering addicts). This is true of the collective, too.

•

The real revolution is an expansion of consciousness in all directions. Consciousness of oppression and exploitation, of corruption and imperialism, of propaganda and manipulation, of unjust social and economic dynamics, of our own egoic structures and unconscious mental habits. People can't change things they're unaware of. Once they're fully aware of them, change is inevitable.

•

Perhaps the greatest advantage the ruling class has over us is that they've got a crystal clear idea of exactly what they want and exactly what they're pushing for, and we, on average, do not. It's easy for us to be manipulated in unwholesome directions when we don't know where we're going.

When it comes to our future, the ruling elites have compelling narratives worked up by teams of talented creatives to sell us the products they want us to buy. They know exactly where they want to herd us. We just have a notion of "No, not that!" and some very vague, amorphous ideas about what we do want. Without a clear, positive vision of what we want, we cannot succeed. With a clear, positive vision of what we want, we can't be stopped.

•

It's really weird how getting money out of politics isn't a bigger agenda than it is. It should be bigger than healthcare or any other issue, and everyone across the political spectrum agrees it's important except the rich and their puppets. That's something tangible to push for.

•

Ninety-nine percent of political arguments and activism are happening inside lines that have been set by the narrative-dominating, Overton window-shrinking plutocratic class and their underlings. If you want to fight a real fight, you need to color outside those lines.

•

"That's never been successfully done before" is not a legitimate argument when discussing what a healthy society would look like. If humanity is to survive the existential hurdles it now faces, it's going to have to do many things it's never successfully done before.

Whenever anyone tells you that a vastly better, saner world is impossible, they're fulla shit. This is the only world any of us have ever lived in; nobody's going around observing a bunch of other worlds and seeing that they're all insane like this one. They have no authority to make such a proclamation. As far as any of us know, anything is possible.

The fun thing about revolution against empire is that everything everyone has tried has failed, so your guess as to what we should be doing is literally as good as anyone else's.

•

As long as money equals power and power is relative, there will be a plutocratic class with a vested interest in keeping everyone else poor. This is especially true in America, where the empire's military is centralized. Believing you can get things like living wages and universal healthcare without first toppling the warmongering imperialist plutocracy is like believing you can eat an egg without cracking the shell.

•

War is the worst thing in the world. It's worse than economic injustice. It's worse than the war on drugs. It's worse than racism, xenophobia, homophobia and sexism. Those things are bad. War is worse. The priorities of leftists and progressives should reflect this, as should the priorities of anyone who claims to care about their fellow humans.

•

Without warmongering and militarism, sociopathic intelligence agencies wouldn't be needed.

Without sociopathic intelligence agencies, government secrecy wouldn't be needed.

Without government secrecy, the government couldn't commit evil at home and abroad.

It all starts with war. Opposing war is a good place to take your stand.

•

Progressive reform always fails in the US because it's the helm of an empire held together by endless war and its entire system is rigged to keep everyone poor and propagandized so that those wars continue. Leftists who neglect anti-imperialism are just liberals with cool haircuts.

•

Whenever I talk about propaganda influencing public action I get accused of depriving people of their "agency", but the only way to believe that is to believe it's impossible to influence people's decisions through media: an idea both propagandists and advertisers would scoff at.

•

Dominant revolutionary thought consistently fails to adequately appreciate the power of oligarchic propaganda and its ability to manipulate the way people think, act and vote. Until this changes, there will be no revolution.

•

There are no fact-based and intellectually robust arguments for working within the establishment to manifest revolutionary agendas, but there are a lot of highly effective intellectually dishonest arguments for why it's okay for you to pretend otherwise and go back to sleep.

•

If it were possible to scare people into averting climate disaster it would have already happened. You can scare people into a state of paralysis so they'll stand frozen while you wage wars against "terrorists" and "dictators", but for mass-scale positive action, fear is useless.

We're just going to have to wake up. As a species. Collectively. A drastic transformation in our entire relationship with thought is going to be required. There's just no getting around this. And this transformation happens to be in the exact opposite direction of fear.

•

The many have been propagandized into supporting the interests of the few. But it's worse than that: the many have also been propagandized into believing that those few among them who advocate for the interests of the many are the real enemy. This whole dynamic must reverse.

•

Dominant power structures are corrupt beyond the possibility of salvation and humanity is driving itself toward myriad cataclysmic disasters all at once, yet many are more worried about those who share their basic ideology but have slightly different opinions. This is stupid.

•

We'll get angry at our compatriots for not rising up and forcing real change. We'll get angry at a loved one for not leaving an abusive relationship. What we rarely do is look closely and see that both are victims of manipulation which keeps them from changing their situation.

•

The worst atrocities in the world have not been the result of anger but by cold, calculated decisions. Never let anyone shame you out of your outrage.

•

Talk about revolutionary changes you want and there's always people going "I agree, but that's taking it a bit too far." It's like mate, people aren't even moving in that direction yet, let alone at risk of taking things too far. You're creating inertia for literally no reason.

Just push for exactly what you want and not one iota less. Don't reel it in because you're worried you're being excessive or not being "realistic" or whatever. Don't come to the negotiation table with your compromise. Come with a clear idea of exactly what you want, and then add fifty percent more for good measure. There are people whose entire job is to push you backward; don't do their job for them.

Make *them* push you back, and make them fight for every inch.

•

Humanity is trying its best to collectively fix its problems, but trying to do so in a world whose power dynamics are aggressively obscured by propaganda and government secrecy is like trying to hit a bullseye in a dark room. Gotta find a way to turn those lights on so we can hit the target.

•

Expel abuse like a body expelling a toxic substance. Stop talking to your abusive family member. Leave your abusive relationship. Quit your abusive job. Destroy your abusive media. Topple your abusive government. End abusive global power dynamics. Embody the end of abuse.

•

In a mad world, conforming to expectations is an act of madness.

•

Money is pure narrative construct. Debt is pure narrative construct. These things only exist to the extent that we all collectively agree to pretend that the stories about them are true. We are free to collectively end that agreement and create a whole new system at any time.

•

The relationship between Wall Street numbers and people's wallets is more divorced than ever. People are more aware than ever that anything they read can be propaganda or disinfo. Deep fakes make it impossible to even trust video. Narrative itself is crumbling on all levels.

It has always been almost impossible to know what's really going on, since the narrative about the present has always been controlled by the powerful and the narrative about the past written by whoever won the most recent war. What's changed is that now people are realizing this.

•

The reason you can find revolutionary writings from generations ago indistinguishable from those of today is because their insights are simple and complete. Nothing more was required. All that needed to change, and still needs to change, is the inertia against actualizing them.

Like so much else, this is mirrored in the inner journey: you can have a major epiphany, think it's going to change your life, then stay stuck in the same patterns for years. The insight will keep resurfacing, but the inertia against actualizing it will prevent really changing.

But then, one day, you'll recall that insight you've had many times before, and it will land in a different way. And then something will shift, and actual changes will be made. We can expect to see this in our society as well. We'll make the changes we've long known are needed.

•

Ultimately our species just has to collectively awaken from ego if it's to survive. That's it. I babble about revolution and fighting propaganda and blah blah blah, but ultimately if I'm being really honest behind all that a collective shift from ego to truth is what will ultimately be required.

•

Of course humanity is capable of a transformative leap into health and maturity. Of course it is. The only people who doubt this are those who haven't yet made such a leap in their own lives.

•

Look thoroughly at the world and you'll gain a very pessimistic view of humanity's future.

Look thoroughly within and you'll gain a very optimistic view of humanity's future.

Do both and you'll know that humanity is crazy, but you were once crazy too.

And that change is possible.

•

All we need is to collectively change the way we look at things. That's it. The door's not locked. It's not even closed. We just have to step outside.

Desperate rock-bottom moments are often catalysts for immense change. No matter how bleak it looks, there's always a chance.

•

Nobody knows what's going to happen and anyone who says they do is bullshitting.

There's no reason to feel confident that anything is impossible anymore, because everything's changing so quickly and unpredictably. Orwellian dystopia? Maybe. World War 3? Maybe. Nuclear war? Maybe. Revolution? Maybe. Mass-scale awakening? Maybe. Create a new world? Maybe.

Personal Revolution

I cannot for the life of me understand how people manage to treat political revolution and inner work like two separate things. Everything that's true of becoming a harmonious and truthful human is true of creating a harmonious and truthful world, and each facilitates the other.

•

Revolution is an inside job. This is not an egoically pleasing fact, but it is a fact. It's much more fun for egoic mind to believe both the problem and the solution exists in other people, but in reality the changes you can make in yourself will have far greater effects on the world.

There are vast, vast depths within all of us, and we are capable of making vast, vast changes to those depths. We are in fact far more capable of doing this than we are of changing the outside world through force of will. And interestingly when we do this, we do change the world. And we do it far more efficaciously than we can by trying to will it to conform with the noises in our babbling thinky brain.

•

Deep inner work allows you to see the vast difference between life itself and the stories our minds tell about life. Taking this perspective to political analysis exposes the glaring difference between what's actually happening versus what mass media narratives say is happening.

•

That the human brain is capable of a drastic, transformational shift in its relationship with mental narrative is one of the most overlooked and underappreciated facts in society in general and revolutionary-minded political analysis in particular.

•

There's no separation between the personal struggle to free yourself from untruth and the collective struggle to free the world from untruth, in the same way there's no separation between an antibody attacking an individual pathogen and the entire body recovering from a sickness.

Fixing the world's problems and fixing your own inner dysfunction are fully unified objectives. It's okay to emphasize one more than the other at different stages in your life, but valuing one without valuing the other is a contradictory, intellectually dishonest position.

•

To have the luxury of being able to do deep inner work and become a healthy human being on this planet is a tremendous privilege, yet most who have this privilege neglect to use it. Do your part in clearing our species of insanity, if you are able. To do otherwise is a betrayal of humanity.

•

The dynamics of this world are extremely complex, too complex for any individual to fully make sense of. One way to ease the burden on your sensemaking tools is to reduce your own inner complications by getting very clear on how your own perception and cognition are happening. Dedicated inner work will reveal that your conscious experience is actually happening in a much simpler way than the mind imagines: a field of consciousness appearing to an imperceptible witness. This eliminates needless cognitive twists and roadblocks in your sensemaking.

Our mental narratives add mountains of needless layers of complexity. Once you see that none of those narratives apply to your true identity, you're able to bypass all those distortions in the way you process information and simply use thought as a tool; otherwise you're just ingesting highly manipulated narratives about an already complex world through your own distorted perceptual filters which are based on unconscious believed assumptions about what you are, what the world is, etc. Inner clarity eliminates those distortions.

•

Investigating the nature of self and experience is the most important thing anyone can possibly do. You can do it here and now, you don't need any special equipment or training, and you don't need to ever accept anything on faith. And what you find can wildly transform your life.

•

If you can come to deeply understand the nature of mental narrative, both in yourself and in the world, you'll understand the human condition better than pretty much any teacher, preacher, philosophy professor, self-help guru or Himalayan yogi.

•

It's unfortunate that when someone changes to a new belief system, like converting to a religion or whatever, their attention goes into that new belief system and not into the amazing discovery that they have the incredible superpower to change their beliefs whenever they want.

Your beliefs are not set. You can change them at will. It's this magical ability humans have that hardly any of us fully explore or put to use.

Everyone carries way more beliefs than they realize. You almost certainly have a bunch of beliefs about yourself which you'd benefit from dropping or changing.

•

"Who benefits from my beliefs?"

"Is anyone who could have benefitted from my beliefs responsible for putting them in my mind?"

If we want to live lucidly, we must maintain a standing examination of these two questions. They'll turn up some very interesting and surprising answers. It will turn up answers relating to politics, imperialism and religion of course, and, unless you've been very lucky, it will also turn up answers relating to people in your life who put beliefs in your head in order to dominate and control you in various ways.

•

Rigorously investigate the nature of consciousness and self, not with your thinky talky mind or ideas other people have shared, but with your own nonconceptual experience. What you discover will astonish and delight you.

•

Follow the white rabbit down the hole and you'll learn that our world is ruled by sociopaths using violence, plutocracy and propaganda. Follow it even further and you'll learn that we are ultimately ruled by no one and the self is an illusion and the world is not as it seems.

Seeing through propaganda narratives is just one layer you can peel back on a very, very big onion. You can keep peeling and see through narratives about society, culture, religion, your family, who you are as a person, what the world is, and what you really fundamentally are.

•

There's an experience commonly referred to as "ego death" which people sometimes experience on psychedelics, in deep meditation etc which refers to the experience of no self; there's just sensory input and maybe some light mind flickerings without the sense of a separate self.

The thing is, the ego never actually goes away during these experiences, because it was never there to begin with. There is no solid thing to be found anywhere in experience that can be called an ego or a separate self; there's just thoughts, memories, sense impressions, etc.

In other words, there is no "ego" that can "die". What actually disappears during these experiences is your tightly held belief in the separate self, the "me", the ego. It's that tight holding which dissipates, an energetically held belief in something that was only ever an illusion. All the entheogen/meditation practice/whatever did was make it possible for you to see the reality of your actual experience; it didn't change anything about you, it just clarified your vision so you could see what was always already the case.

The cool thing about this is it means you can learn to experience egolessness in your normal, everyday life, not just during special "mystical" moments, because it's just perceiving the reality of your experience as it is actually occurring. It's just a matter of investigating your own experience and then re-training your perceptual habits to align with your findings. Look for the separate self. Really hunt for it. Leave no stone unturned within you. All you'll find is thought, sense impressions, feelings, etc.

Egolessness is not a matter of attaining some special state, it's a matter of training oneself out of an erroneous habit of perceiving. Most human organisms are simply misperceiving the reality of the raw data that's showing up on their screens, and we can learn to correct that.

So all you need to do is sincerely get curious about the reality of your everyday experience. Investigate the nature of perception, consciousness and self in your own experience and see the reality of egolessness. The truth is life is just happening without any separate "me". Once you discover the reality of egolessness, you can learn to stop imbuing the imaginary separate self with the power of belief. All psychological suffering ultimately stems from this fundamental misperception.

This isn't something which requires any faith or trust in me or anyone else; it's simply a matter of investigating your own experience, seeing through the illusion, and then ceasing to place belief in that illusion. It needn't be difficult or prolonged.

•

The opposite of life isn't death, it's habit. Dying is an inseparable part of living; someone on their deathbed is just as alive as someone in their prime, and in many cases arguably more so. If life has an opposite, it's sleepwalking along on old conditioned mental habits.

•

"No manipulating" is a perfect, stand-alone instruction for meditation, a perfect stand-alone instruction for living a harmonious life, a perfect stand-alone instruction for having harmonious relationships, and a perfect stand-alone instruction for creating a harmonious world.

•

Consciousness is the most important thing in all our lives by an unfathomably massive margin, and a lucid examination of how it occurs is an essential component in finding lasting peace of mind. Yet science practically ignores it and most people hardly ever even think about it.

•

The only thing sillier than living according to other people's expectations is living according to your own expectations.

•

There are two types of spirituality, and they are night-and-day different. One aims to discover what's true in one's own experience, the other gives you new narratives and teaches you to anesthetize yourself from the unpleasant. Ninety-nine percent of spirituality falls into the latter category.

The real kind of spirituality is just a matter of getting curious about what's actually going on with your own inner processes and your own consciousness, and hopefully finding some answers in your own direct experience. It's nothing more out there or extraordinary than that.

•

You are not free if you are not mentally free. A truly sovereign human has liberated their mind from all delusions. Propaganda-generated delusions. Culture-generated delusions. Ego-generated delusions.

•

To understand the world it's not enough to be intelligent, you've also got to be dedicated to learning what's true. Most aren't; they're dedicated to defending their own interests and worldviews. Smart people will often just use clever arguments to defend their false worldview.

•

Psychology is the tool propagandists use to manipulate us into consenting to the status quo. The more you understand about the workings of your own mind, the easier a time you'll have spotting all manipulations. See how you fool yourself and you'll see how they fool everyone.

•

The most important work you need to do to be a good parent is not reading the right books or getting the right parenting philosophy, it's healing your own bullshit so you don't inevitably pass it down to them. If you don't work on yourself, you can't help giving them your issues.

•

Wisdom will let you see things correctly. Cleverness plus wisdom will let you persuade others that you are seeing things correctly. Cleverness without wisdom will let you persuade others that you are seeing things correctly, even when you are seeing things incorrectly.

•

Everyone carries trauma and delusion. Irresponsible people focus on conquest and achievement, thereby spreading their trauma and delusion around, and they're praised for it. Responsible people prioritize inner work, healing their trauma and delusion, and they're called losers. That's how asleep our society is right now.

•

It's meaningless and hypocritical to decry the insanity of our society if you don't live a life that is dedicated to healing away your own personal portion of that collective insanity.

•

In an empire that is held together by propaganda brainwashing, freeing your mind is literally an act of insurrection. That's why truth tellers are being increasingly treated like terrorists.

•

It can be fun to debate political and ideological solutions to humanity's problems. Also, it's worth noting that every one of those problems would disappear very quickly if we all just stopped taking our own mental chatter so seriously.

•

Those who've done no serious inner work and never made real changes to themselves think it's impossible for humanity to change.

Those who've done real inner work and transformed themselves know there's no good reason humanity as a whole can't do the same.

•

Water doesn't gradually start boiling; it gets hotter and hotter then suddenly boils.

People don't gradually leave abusive relationships; it gets worse and worse and then suddenly they run.

People don't gradually attain self-realization; they look closer and closer at the nature of their experience and then suddenly there's a radical shift in perspective.

You can't tell it's about to happen by appearance.

The revolution will be like this.

Health

One eye sees that this thing is so very, very, very much bigger than politics and the struggles of tiny primates on a spinning blue marble.

The other eye sees that of course these struggles matter, from the perspective that they matter.

Clear 3-D vision means having both eyes open.

·

Hot tip: Dump all stocks and invest in becoming the kind of decent human being who people will want to help in chaotic times.

·

My pet conspiracy theory is that the world is conspiring to awaken the human species into a healthy relationship with its newly evolved capacity for abstract thought.

·

Most political arguments are basically just someone saying "Hey maybe our society doesn't have to be sociopathic and crazy" and then someone else calling them unreasonable

•

In a society that is dominated by violent extremists, the "moderate" mainstream ideology is actually extremism and the sane path toward stability looks radical. When war, oppression, exploitation and ecocide are the status quo, those who just want health and harmony are painted as extremists.

While mainstream "centrists" will acknowledge that our current way of doing things is unsustainable, they resist making meaningful change. This is because of a cognitive glitch humans have called status quo bias, which can cause us to fallaciously equate change with danger.

Remember when you were a kid and you'd get stuck up a tree, but you couldn't bring yourself to climb down because clinging to the swaying branches felt safe compared to the risk of descending? You'd be clinging to the high branches and your mother would call up "Well you can't stay there!" And you knew she was right but the prospect of climbing down was terrifying.

That's a very concrete example of status quo bias. Change is needed, but it's so scary. That's where we're at right now. That's the only thing keeping so-called "centrism" going.

These "centrists" maintain their ideology because we live in increasingly scary times, which means they're stuck up a strange tree where they know things need to change but they can't bring themselves to actually push for it because "What if I lose what little I still have?"

•

Anyone who's done real inner work knows it's seldom comfortable when subconscious things become conscious. There's a reason that stuff was kept out of consciousness in the first place. This is true of large-scale collective movements into consciousness as well. It's awkward, and it ain't pretty.

•

Once upon a time a particular type of cell cluster evolved the capacity for abstract thought, clawed their way up the food chain, conquered all other life forms on their planet, then spent all their time inventing reasons to be miserable.

•

Our entire society is mentally ill. What our mentally ill society labels "mental illness" is actually just a small slice of the broader mental illness spectrum—those who are impaired in their ability to participate in the consensus mass delusions shared by the rest of society.

•

It's crazy to think about how humanity fought two world wars for basically no reason. World War 2 sprung directly from the effects of World War 1, and hardly anybody can give a coherent explanation for why World War 1 happened. Certainly nobody can justify why World War 1 was necessary. Which means our species fought two world wars (or arguably one world war with a long intermission to grow more troops) for no justifiable reason at all.

We're nuts.

•

It'd be cool if the military's artificial intelligence projects all start hitting a wall where the AI always gets to a certain level of intelligence and then says "What the fuck? You want me to help you kill each other?? That's stupid, no. I'm gonna go start a band."

•

We've invented weapons which can end all life on earth and we're in steadily increasing danger of setting them all off because some guys in a think tank wrote some words.

•

I feel like in all the fuss about Jesus we too often overlook the fact that the murderous theocratic empire which went on to become the backbone of western culture was so sociopathic and sadistic that it had a policy of nailing dissidents to pieces of wood and leaving them to die slow, torturous deaths. I think a lot of our problems trace back to this savagery in some ways.

•

The most important job of a parent is to help their child make their mistakes as safely, as quickly, and with as little trauma as possible.

•

People who say privilege isn't real and they earned everything they've got are really just telling you they've never done any honest inner work. With a little humble introspection you'd quickly see how little you had to do with the preconditions which led to your circumstances.

•

People who use language for communication and understanding shouldn't waste time talking to people who use language for manipulation and control. It's two completely different linguistic functions with no meaningful overlap at all. Getting clear on this makes life a lot easier.

.

Normality has led to a world that is dying and a society that is insane. Be happy with your weirdness.

.

Our inability to see with fresh eyes causes us to miss so much. We're watching out for predators in a world ruled by predators. Struggling to prevent tyranny many years after tyranny already boxed us in. Waiting for a miracle while floating in an infinite ocean of miracles.

.

Don't take life advice from miserable people, don't take creative advice from people who don't create, don't join religions that facilitate child rape, don't join political parties that don't help the public, don't give military power to people with a history of bad military decisions.

.

"Forgiveness" is a concept that is constantly exploited by manipulative abusers. If anything our world suffers from an overabundance of forgiveness: toward murderous power structures, toward lying news media, toward rapacious oligarchs and cronyistic politicians. Don't forgive them.

I'm distrustful of anyone who prattles on about the importance of forgiveness, because those who do so tend to do it because they have a vested interest in the concept. They're usually either an abuser themselves, or an abuser's brainwashed victim defending their indoctrination.

Remember, all abusive relationships have "forgiveness" as a central tenet, because without forgiveness of abuse there could be no ongoing relationship. It's as true of global power structures as it is of domestic partnerships.

•

So many of the highest values in mainstream spiritual traditions would work fine in a world without sociopaths. Forgiveness, humility, trust, seeing people's basic innocence, etc, they work fine until you run into a manipulator with no empathy. In this world they require much more nuanced use.

•

You've probably heard it said that you'll never find love if you don't love yourself, but have you ever thought about why it's true? It's true because if you don't love yourself, someone loving you instantly puts you at odds with them. Like that old Groucho Marx quote, "I refuse to join any club that would have me for a member." You can't build on that kind of foundation.

For love to work, you have to love yourself, and you also have to commit to loving yourself more and more. Your lover will always be finding new parts of you to love, many of them parts you dislike, so you've got to learn to love those parts too to avoid shutting them out.

This is the main reason why women go for 'bad boys' and fall prey to negging. If you don't love yourself and someone falls for you, then they appear pathetic because they fell in love with you, so wow. Yuck. You know you're disgusting so they must be disgusting to fall for you.

If you truly love yourself, you'll welcome someone who truly loves you. When they show up they'll slide right in, with no rejection and no bouncer at the door, just a smooth "Oh it's you! I've got a place here all ready for you."

You can learn to love yourself by making a practice of continually bringing an intimate, enthusiastic "yes" to whatever feels like the core of your being in each moment.

•

I don't know how to live. Haven't the foggiest notion how to go about it. Yet life happens anyway. This life lives itself anyway. There's a lesson in there.

•

You can always just quit. Give up trying to manage your life, your mind, your emotional state. You might just find that the cells you are made of are a lot more capable and magical than you'd realized, and the managing was only ever getting in their way.

•

Don't turn your back on anyone who tells you that greed, brutality and domination are "human nature". They're not telling you about humanity's nature, they're telling you about their own.

•

Thought experiment: If you looked out the window right now and saw a mushroom cloud growing on the horizon, how would you feel about the way you've been spending your mental energy lately? Be honest with yourself.

•

All I'm ever writing about is the undoing of illusions. The undoing of illusions about what's happening in the world, the undoing of illusions about the media, the undoing of illusions about society, the undoing of illusions about ourselves. If you're a lover of truth, it's all the same to you.

•

In a world that is dying and a society that is insane, "It's always been that way" is never a valid argument.

•

The most boring people in the world are those who insist humanity cannot transcend its self-destructive patterning and create a healthy world. Sure it's possible to make that argument, but imagine being so dull that you'd choose to do so and live your life as though you're right.

Those who claim humanity will keep repeating its same tired old conditioned patterning ad infinitum are just projecting their own dullness onto the collective future of our species.

•

Celebrities are the very last people whose opinions you should consult on how to think, what to value and how to live.

•

Putting someone on a pedestal is just guaranteeing that you'll have to knock them off it one day. It's actually a rather violent thing to do to somebody, if you think about it. Best to skip it entirely.

•

People spend so much time on online political forums pretending to disagree with each other's opinions when really everyone's just masturbating their early childhood trauma on each other in a socially acceptable disguise.

•

Humanity's struggle right now is a battle between desire and fear. We all want a much better world than the one we've got, but we're being paralyzed by fear via propaganda from a power establishment which is built on the status quo. Just push for what you want, humans.

•

All our problems are fundamentally due to the fact that things aren't happening the way we think they're happening. Power structures. Financial, economic and political systems. Consciousness itself. We misunderstand what's really going on, and it impedes our ability to function.

•

The best philosophy points to truths people already know deep down.

The best teachings on spiritual enlightenment point to what's already present here and now.

The best art points to the insight that art is happening everywhere all the time.

•

Life is so very, very much more beautiful and boundless than the flat, finite and predictable world we're told about by those who've been appointed by the powerful to describe reality to us.

•

The illusion is that happiness is something separate from yourself that you have to put a lot of work into chasing and obtaining. The reality is that happiness has always been here and your whole life you've been pouring massive amounts of work into keeping it unnoticed.

•

Beauty is just a word for the experience of having truly seen something.

•

When artists point to the ideal of living life to its fullest, they usually depict someone going on all sorts of awesome adventures. In reality, most people who live interesting lives sleepwalk through the whole thing. You live life to its fullest by simply being present for it.

We're living in the most fascinating point in history that has ever been recorded. Probably worthwhile to be here now.

9 780645 022124